# Popular Management Books

The growing interest in management knowledge has generated an enormous literature. Popular Management Books offers a number of American management gurus and provides a timely and radical critique of the management discourse offered by popular management books. Features include:

* Detailed examination of the sociological trajectory of North American management discourse;

* An examination of books by leading popular management gurus such as Tom Peters, Richard Normann and Robert Waterman;

* An investigation into the creation, diffusion and consumption of management knowledge;

* The implications for organisations of acting on popular management discourse.

*Popular Management Books* is a much needed corrective to the under-researched criticism of mass management books.

Staffan Furusten is Assistant Professor at the Stockholm School of Economics and the Stockholm Centre for Organisational Research.

# Popular Management Books

## How they are made and what they mean for organisations

## Staffan Furusten

London and New York

First published 1999
by Routledge
11 New Fetter Lane, London EC4P 4EE

Simultaneously published in the USA and Canada
by Routledge
29 West 35th Street, New York, NY 10001

*Routledge Ltd is an imprint of the Taylor & Francis Group*

© 1999 Staffan Furusten

Typeset in Garamond by Routledge
Printed and bound in Great Britain by Biddles Ltd, Guildford
and King's Lynn

*British Library Cataloguing in Publication Data*
A catalogue record is available from the British Library

*Library of Congress Cataloging in Publication Data*
Popular management books: how they are made and what
they mean for organisations/Staffan Furusten.
An English adaptation from the Swedish title: Den
populära managementkulturen.
Includes bibliographical references and index.
1. Management literature. I. Title.
HD31.F8713   1999
99–18144          658–dc21                CIP

ISBN 0–415–21218–9 (hbk)
ISBN 4–415–21219–7 (pbk)

To Kristina, Axel and Ernst

# Contents

# Illustrations

# Preface

This is a book about popular management books. I am a scholar and the book is written in an academic tradition. However, since its subject is familiar to a vast number of people, there may be readers from different backgrounds, whether students, researchers, management consultants, journalists, managers, human resource managers, managers-to-be or politicians, who for different reasons may find this book interesting.

But it may also be of interest for those who do not have a particular interest in management knowledge, since the book also discusses relations between organisations and their environment, managerial discourses, and the institutional environment of organisations. Who manages whom, and what governs what in such relations? Another discussion touches on how popularisations of management knowledge can be viewed. Yet another discussion that might be of wider interest concerns what generally constitutes knowledge in social science, and how this knowledge is created and can be moved in time and space, although the case in focus is the field of management studies.

The research project reported in this book was initiated in September 1989. Parts of the work have been presented and discussed at seminars and international conferences over the years. Some chapters have also been published elsewhere, in other versions. A first version in English of this book was published in 1995 when I defended my doctoral dissertation at the Department of Business Studies at Uppsala University. A slightly revised version in Swedish was published in 1996 by Nerenius & Santérus Förlag. The translation of the first version into Swedish was initiated by the interest shown from beyond the academic community, from business, media and practitioners in organisations. The Swedish version of the book was met with even greater interest. In parallel, the research field in focus here – the creation and diffusion of management knowledge – has grown. In

1989, when the project reported in this book began, not many studies had focused on these issues. However, several studies have been published during the last couple of years, and there are quite a few in production. These two circumstances, together with the fact that the first English version of the book would soon be out of print, made me consider a revised version in English. This new version is not a translation of the revised Swedish version. All chapters have been revised and updated, and some are now more or less new versions. Moreover, this book should not be seen as a popularisation of academically oriented research, although I have tried not to make the text more complicated than necessary. I therefore hope the present version is more tangible and more precise than both the original English and the later Swedish versions. For these reasons I hope that not only academics and students will find it worthwhile to read.

# Acknowledgements

As the author of this book I take full responsibility for the words, interpretations and arguments presented herein. However, the actual writing of this text (and all others) is the product of a history in a particular social context. Such contexts are impossible to represent in every detail and I therefore address this acknowledgement to a few individuals who have been of particular importance in mine.

Nils Kinch encouraged me to consider an academic career and also suggested the subject of this book. Moreover, he read and commented on almost every sentence I wrote from my first fumbling efforts in 1989 to the last full stop of the original version of this book in 1995. Furthermore, I derived much benefit from the supervision, encouragement and comments offered by Lars Engwall over the years. I am greatly indebted to Lars for our intense discussions on the development of my project and in the completion of the first version of this book. By constructively refusing to understand, both Nils and Lars also compelled me to make many inconvenient but necessary changes. I am very grateful for their patience and constructive criticism.

Among the other members of the Department of Business Studies at Uppsala University, where the original study was carried out, I am in different ways particularly grateful to Kent Eriksson, Sven Jungerhem, Rolf Marquardt, Hans Hasselbladh, Carin B. Ericsson, Leif Arnesson, Jannis Kallinikos, Ingemund Hägg, Lee Jong-Woo, Konstantin Lampou, Jan Lindvall, Mats Nordström, Peter Thilenius, C-G. Thunman, Deo Sharma and Fotis Theodoridis.

A group of people outside the Department supplied valuable assistance. Barbara Czarniawska has served me with suggestions at different stages of this project and has also given detailed and constructive comments as the discussant when I defended both my licentiate and doctoral dissertations. John Meyer read and commented on two different manuscripts thereof, and Robert Cooper gave creative suggestions on how to develop my project further at an early stage. I am also indebted to Brian Bloomfield and Hugh Willmott for their helpful suggestions and advice. In completing the first version of this book I also benefited from a discussion with Richard Whitley. José Luis Alvarez also gave me well informed comments on a few papers. I am also indebted to Lars Albert, who constructively criticised different manuscripts. Special thanks go to Richard Normann, who generously answered my questions and also commented on parts of this manuscript. Without the suggestions and comments from these people, certain important steps would never have been taken.

In completing the project that was first reported on in my doctoral dissertation in 1995, I owe a great debt to Nils Brunsson and Kerstin Sahlin-Andersson, who at a late stage in my doctoral studies invited me to join their research group at the Stockholm School of Economics and at SCORE (Stockholm Centre for Organisational Research). The inspiring and constructive research atmosphere at SCORE has made me realise the weaknesses of the earlier versions of this book. Unfortunately I have not been able to deal with all of them in this book, but the theoretical parts and the conclusions in particular have been updated, based largely on discussions with all my colleagues at SCORE.

Moreover, without the financial support of the Department of Business Studies and the Faculty of Social Science at Uppsala University, Kungliga Vetenskapsakademin, Wahlgrenska Stiftelsen, Christer Berch and E.E:son's donor, HSFR, the Economic Research Institute at Stockholm School of Economics, Tore Browalds and Jan Wallanders research scholarships, and the Council for Research on Working Life issues, it would have been impossible to make this study and complete this new version of the book.

Staffan Furusten
Uppsala, December 1998

# 1 A study of popular management books

## A growing interest in management knowledge in the 1980s

Since the early 1980s there has been a growing interest in management knowledge in the western world. This has taken many forms. Special sections on management are published in newspapers, and American business magazines like the *Harvard Business Review*, *Fortune* and *Business Week* are disseminated worldwide. Moreover, a number of local business journals appear in many countries. These magazines cover the fads and the popular practically oriented development in the broad field of managerial knowledge. Another feature is an increasing number of seminars and short courses on management-related issues which are arranged inside companies and offered on the market. These are of various kinds, some being connected to business schools and universities and organised as management development programmes mainly based on academic research; others are more spectacular, where for example clergymen and actors have been engaged to give lectures. Programmes are also devised, based on psychology and oriental mysticism, to help people become familiar with their 'inner energy' and build up their self-confidence. Furthermore, the market for various kinds of management consultancy has grown, where the supply varies from offering adventurous tours for top management to conducting sophisticated clinical analyses of organisations' problems followed by suggestions, advice and support on how to cure them. Concerning the latter kind of consultancy, a pre-eminent feature during the 1980s was the increasing worldwide activities pursued by, in particular, American-based consulting firms like Arthur Andersen & Co., the Boston Consulting Group, and McKinsey & Co. These endeavours have continued and escalated in the 1990s.

But the most obvious occurrence of the increased interest in manifestations of management and leadership is perhaps the popularity of statements by great management thinkers like Peter Drucker, Kenneth Blanchard, Henry Mintzberg, Rosabeth Moss-Kanter, Tom Peters and Michael Porter. These thinkers, or gurus, as Kennedy (1991) and Huczynski (1993) prefer to call them, travel around the world and give lectures and executive seminars. In recent years, advances in multimedia technology have enabled them to give live video performances broadcast simultaneously to several places. This has been practised by those such as Michael Porter, Peter Drucker and Tom Peters, and it means that gurus can now give lectures from home which can be attended by several audiences in different cities and countries all over the world. These seminars are organised as ordinary executive live performances where people pay fees to listen to the guru even though they will only meet him or her on a video screen. As at conventional seminars, there is also time for questions after the performance, where the global audience can fax questions to be answered live by the speaker (Jackson 1994).

According to Huczynski (1993: 4–5), Blanchard, Mintzberg, Moss-Kanter and Porter can be characterised as modern business-school academics, while Peters is seen as a management consultant. It also seems fair to assign the grand old man of management gurus, Peter Drucker, to the first category. Closely related to this feature of contemporary western society are the books which these gurus have written. A substantial element in achieving worldwide guru status consists in the production of books which reach considerable sales volumes (cf. Huczynski 1993: 230). The most obvious example in this case is probably Tom Peters, whose book *In Search of Excellence* (1982), written jointly with Robert Waterman, sold close to a million copies within a year, and by 1988 was said to have sold over ten million copies worldwide (Thomas 1989).[1] Even today, in the late 1990s, it is well known and read by researchers, students and practitioners. It also is one of the most cited books in the field of management studies (Engwall 1998). In this regard it can be seen as a classic of management literature. Peters is presented by Kennedy (1991) as the guru of gurus, since he has continued to write books which have become bestsellers even though they have not sold as well as *In Search of Excellence*. He has also made great efforts in travelling around the world and holding seminars ever since the publication of the 1982 book. But he is not alone in this business, although he was one of the first to gain a global reputation; among many others, the authors of the bestselling *Reengineering the Corpora-*

*tion; A Manifesto for Business Revolution* (Hammer and Champy 1993) can be seen as recent rising stars.

However, yet another major category of bestselling authors is mentioned by Huczynski, namely well known chief executives like Jan Carlzon (1985; 1987), Harold Geneen (1985), Lee Iacocca (1984), Mark McCormack (1984) and John Sculley (1987), all of whom have written career autobiographies detailing how they, or the organisations which they managed, made successful turnarounds or attained remarkable success in a short period. In the 1990s we have seen fewer books written by this category of author, yet successful managers continue to be valued speakers at management seminars and other large events.

The phenomenon outlined above is the starting point for this study. The focus is on the 1980s, since this was a dramatic period in the globalisation of popular management culture, manifested by gurus with million-selling books and worldwide seminar tours. Although the 1980s was a spectacular period, the phenomenon as such was not new, and is still remarkable in the late 1990s. As implied by Barley and Kunda (1992) in their study of the development of the American managerial discourse from the late nineteenth century until the early 1990s, the rise of new ideas and changes in the principal ideologies, and the dissemination of these, can be traced back to important oral (speeches and lectures) and written (articles and books) presentations by a few individuals, certain groups at business schools (mainly at Harvard), and a few consulting firms and business magazines. Furthermore, texts written by gurus often appear as overt (explicit) or underlying (implicit) references in articles in business journals, in literature used in management development programmes, and in other popular books (cf. Kennedy 1991). However, such texts also appear in courses at universities and business schools, as important references for consultants (cf. Furusten and Kinch 1996) and in academic research (cf. Engwall 1994). Although the gurus may advocate different perspectives and suggest different models for solving organisational and managerial problems, it is still true that what a few gurus articulate is disseminated to a vast number of people in the world through the various distribution channels of modern society. To conclude, it should be noted that the supply of managerial manifestations both in the past and today seems to be dominated by services offered by a few consulting firms, a few management books, a few management gurus, a few business magazines, and a few management development programmes. Moreover, it has been noted that most of them originate from Boston (Bjørkman 1997).

This book puts popular management books in focus and addresses the question of how they are produced and what they mean for organisations. The analyses are illustrated primarily by examples from the 1980s. However, although the 1980s was an interesting period, it is not this period as such this book wants to examine. The 1980s is significant because of the boom of an international popular management culture, but when it comes to the questions raised here, examples could just as well have been selected from the early twentieth century when the ideas of Frederic Taylor were first set in print, or the 1930s when Chester Barnard wrote his seminal work, or the 1950s when several books were published in areas such as human relations, or the 1990s when the concept of Business Process Re-engineering spread across the globe, primarily promoted by Hammer and Champy's (1993) book. Rather than comment on the production of popular management books during this century as a whole, which has been done elsewhere (e.g. McGill 1988; Barley and Kunda 1992; Huzcynski 1993) this book concentrates on a limited time period. This limitation makes it possible to go deeper into the processes whereby popular management books are produced, and the analysis of their production.

## Popular managerial manifestations as elements of the organisational environment

The phenomenon discussed above appeared on a worldwide scene, and the scenario was organisational and managerial life. This means that activities by people who supply ideas, advice and education on how organisations work and should be managed take place in environments of organisations. Moreover, due to the fact that just a few consulting firms, books, business magazines, management development programmes, etc. reach considerable popularity, there are reasons to believe that these have a major influence on how individuals and organisations in modern society apprehend and make enactments of their reality. In other words, due to the wide diffusion of a few particular manifestations, they can be seen as important carriers of representations of managerial and organisational life in contemporary global society. If this holds true it is very important to know what they carry, since they thereby may represent ideas that a great deal of individuals in modern western society are most likely to refer to when they make enactments of the reality in organisations. Moreover, as argued by e.g. Weick (1979a), these enactments are important for the reality they observe as well as the choices and actions they make. This would mean that popular managerial manifestations are powerful elements that contribute to the isomorphism of ideas about managerial and organisational reality in the western world, and thereby perhaps also of individual and collective choices and actions. If north American gurus and management consultants are as important in the worldwide managerial discourse as the discussion above intimates, then this phenomenon can be seen as somewhat of an American crusade of managerial ideas. This would imply that when people in for example Sweden, the UK, Italy and other western countries make enactments of organisation and management, they primarily refer to ideas emanating from north America.

This study is devoted to an analysis of the popularity of managerial manifestations. However, it is a broad topic and we therefore focus on a more narrow aspect of the phenomenon. In particular the purpose here is to study what popular management books represent as elements in the environments of organisations. Can they, for instance, be character-ised as representing, and thereby carrying, knowledge; are they on the other hand more likely to be defined as carriers of myths, institutions, beliefs, and ideologies; or do they tend to be a mixture of the two? Moreover, what do they mean for organisations? By seeking to identify the characteristics of the production and supply of popular management books, my intention is that the analyses and discussions throughout the book will, if not answer these questions comprehensively, at least suggest possible explanations of just what it is that popular managerial manifestations – such as books – carry between organisations and societies. Even though this is important to know, it is very complex to investigate. Therefore we shall identify below a few aspects of particular importance in the discussions to follow. It will not be possible in one study to make empirical observations on all, but by observing a few it will be possible to elaborate theoretically on the others.

### From the production of popular managerial manifestations to their consumption by organisations

So far we have noted that in this book popular managerial manifestations are seen as elements in environments of organisations. In fact they are regarded as packages that articulate and thereby carry knowledge, ideologies, norms, values, notions, standards and institutions of managerial and organisational life between individuals, organisations and societies. Following Scott and Meyer (1983; 1991) these kinds of environmental elements belong in the institutional environment of organisations. This means that they contribute to the social construction of reality both in organisations and in the wider society. Thus they are of some importance for our concepts of what organisations are and how they can be managed. In this way they can be seen as constituents of social mechanisms that together with, for example, laws and regulations made by governments and business trade associations, create and govern the institutional rules and conventions (cf. Meyer 1994) of managerial and organisational life in a modern society.

Figure 1.1 seeks to demonstrate that popular management books are elements in a debate that takes place in the institutional environments of organisations. People who create, diffuse and consume popular management books constitute what in this study we call the general managerial discourse. The figure also illustrates how the concepts mentioned above are believed to be related, namely that there is an interrelationship between the consumption of management books in organisations and the production and diffusion thereof. Thus popular management books are voices in the general managerial discourse, which is, in its turn, a layer in the institutional environments of organisations which is also an element in the more general environment of organisations.

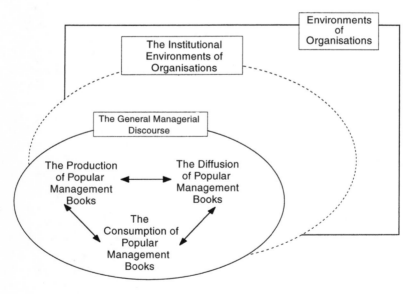

*Figure 1.1*   The environments of organisations and the production, diffusion and consumption of managerial manifestations

This environment can then be seen as embedded in modern society, although it is not illustrated in the figure.

The figure is intended to illustrate the discussions to come in later chapters of this book; however, it is important to note here that the processes represented by the different concepts in the figure are taking place simultaneously. In other words, events occur in society and in organisational environments at the same time as management books are consumed in organisations and produced and diffused by others in their environments. Thus the relationship between the production of popular management books and the consumption thereof in organisations may not follow the common view. In other words, it might not be that an individual first observes something and then reports it in, for example, a book which in the next step is diffused to a consumer who then consumes it. The reverse may very well be true, where the consumer in one way or another communicates what he likes to consume to the creator, who then produces this to please him. But this is an empirical question which will be discussed more thoroughly later in this book, when the characteristics of the supply and production of popular management books are discussed.

## Some limitations of the study

What popular management books represent as elements in the environments of organisations is a broad topic and difficult to investigate. The analyses must therefore be limited to a few tangible aspects. One limitation has already been stated inasmuch as the purpose should be fulfilled by searching for characteristics of the supply and production of popular management books. Thus this study is confined to popular books as such, ignoring their application in organisations. However, these applications will be discussed in terms of the consumption of managerial manifestations, where we start with the findings from empirical observations of their characteristics. Similar complexities have been in focus elsewhere and it is thereby possible to draw upon earlier studies which discussed both the application of knowledge and the relation between elements in the institutional environments of organisations and local organisational processes.

Another delimitation derives from the difficulties inherent in a comprehensive study of all kinds of managerial manifestations. Therefore we shall here focus on popular management books, since these can be seen as significant elements in the popular managerial discourse. In other words, popular management books describe aspects of managerial life and are as such likely to be connected to many other situations where popular managerial manifestations are formulated.

Consequently, the explicit purpose of this study can be described as a search for characteristics of the supply and production of popular management books in order to define the characteristics of the popular managerial discourse. It will then be possible to discuss theoretically the relations between the production, diffusion and consumption of popular managerial manifestations. This will then enable us to draw conclusions as to what the contents of popular management books are, and what they represent as elements in the organisational environment. We can then go on to discuss the implications for organisations when popular managerial manifestations are consumed therein: namely what they mean for organisations.

## Earlier studies of popularised management knowledge

Few studies are to be found where popular management books are selected as empirical objects and analysed as elements of the organisational environment. Nevertheless, several studies have discussed the popularity of management issues, and in order to clarify the purpose of the present study it is therefore important to compare it to a selection of these previous investigations.

The popularity of managerial manifestations is mentioned in many studies, although very few have dealt with it explicitly. Nevertheless, McGill (1988) for instance, attempts to expose modern management myths. He maintains that the predominant assumptions in modern society are presented as quick fixes, i.e. particular models and methods are supposed to be applied to complex organisational problems as instant remedies which will blow all the problems away. His concern is that the vast supply of such quick fixes has resulted in a 'managerial morass wherein simplistic solutions take form, flower briefly, then sink back to feed new forms' (ibid.: 6). The major conclusion he draws is that the mythical quick fixes do not correspond with the reality which surrounds managers, and therefore obstruct the understanding of the real complexities of management (ibid.: 220–1). Although he argues that in times of distress and uncertainty myths can provide comfort and guidance, he holds that the mythology of management has 'drawn managers away from the realities of modern management and fixed them in patterns of feeling and thought that are inappropriate to contemporary organizational life' (ibid.: 202).

According to McGill, the predominant modern managerial myths represent a 'wrong' view of organisational and managerial life. He also implies that there is a 'right' view, even though he does not state it. However, the differentiation of 'right' from 'wrong' representations of organisational and managerial life is not unproblematic, particularly if we apply a social constructive approach to knowledge (cf. Berger and Luckmann 1967). This approach is one of the major points of departure of the present study and is discussed in detail in Chapter 3. However, it may be appropriate at this point to briefly clarify how this approach differs from McGill's. In other words, according to Berger and Luckmann, the meaning of reality and 'knowledge of reality' are not natural objects, but rather results of particular social processes where individuals interact and negotiate to reach socially accepted agreements on assumptions which are supposed to be real. Consequently, what is experienced as real is socially constructed, and what is believed to be right in one social network may be seen as wrong in another, and vice-versa. It is therefore hazardous to introduce the predominant manifestations as incorrect descriptions of organisational and managerial life. It might be appropriate to do so in some situations and social networks but, as pointed out by Czarniawska-Joerges (1988), what is most wrong might sometimes be what causes the best actions, i.e. the wrong myth could act as a metaphor which encourages people to make important moves that otherwise would not have occurred.

Huczynski's (1993) examination of management gurus is another relevant study which explicitly discusses the wide popularity of managerial manifestations. His major concern is to determine why certain ideas are so attractive and confer extremely high rewards on the management gurus who develop and present them (2). His main conclusions are that the idea must be timely, be brought to the attention of its potential audience, meet organisational requirements and individual needs, and be attractively articulated (1). These conclusions are hardly surprising: his identification of management gurus over time is, however, of more interest, together with his comments that the development of management studies over the last hundred years can be divided into six major families of ideas, and that some themes recur in all of these.[2] He discusses the development and diffusion of these ideas over time and says, for instance, that many of the popular ideas in the 1980s represented 'old wine in new bottles' (210). Furthermore, that these families of ideas constitute somewhat of an 'intellectual bank from which the producers of management ideas make withdrawals in order to produce what, ultimately, may become the management fad of the future' (269). However, Huczynski's study is most likely to be seen as a presentation of empirical observations on management thinkers whose books have been widely distributed over time. In other words, he does not present a structured analysis and discussion of the implications of his findings. He rather describes different aspects of management ideas which have been popular over time (e.g. who the gurus are, which ideas have become popular, particular circumstances of the periods when the most popular books were written, efforts at promotion and how texts and speeches are presented in public, and the prevalence of particular fads and fashions at different times). The crucial differences between Huczynski's and the present study pertain to the creation of popular texts; thus we seek here to discuss and analyse the empirical observations in closer relation to theoretical achievements reported in other related studies.

In another study, Barley and Kunda (1992) analyse the development of the American managerial discourse from the late nineteenth century to the present.[3] They do not explicitly discuss the popularity of management ideas, but these provide the theme of their argument. They identify a few social conditions and a few categories of voices (in some cases even particular individuals) which have played crucial roles when the focus of the discourse shifted. Thus they maintain that although the dominant perspective has changed, this does not mean that former dominant perspectives have been superseded. These are still parts of the general discourse, but the prominence has shifted (cf. Huczynski 1993). They also say that each shift in dominance of perspectives (or ideologies as they call them) also involved a shift from normative to rational rhetoric, the next shift being from rational to normative, and so on. By rational they mean that there is a tendency in the rhetoric clearly to structure the arguments into cause-and-effect relations, while by normative they mean an encouraging rhetoric which consists of how things should be and how people should behave.

Their overall aim is to describe the development and explain why new ideologies have emerged and displaced earlier dominant ideologies. They therefore mention a number of conditions in the world of organisations which were probably crucial. Thus all changes in perspective tend to be related to the fact that practitioners began to search for other methods of controlling an increasing organisational complexity in times of dramatic or rapid changes in their environment. These changes, namely the forces which prompted the practitioners to search for new ways of organising and controlling organisations, could be social, political or technical in character. Throughout the period covered by Barley and Kunda, this search was encountered by researchers and teachers at business schools (predominantly Harvard), who wrote books and articles and presented public lectures and seminars. Other important contributors, they point out, were those who founded specific societies concerned with particular streams of thought, for example scientific management and human relations, and those who founded consulting firms. The latter, that is, consultants who offered their services on the market, together with popular business magazines and books, are described by Barley and Kunda as probably the most important group of voices in the development of new ideologies from the 1950s onward. Thus they also mention governmental war-related commissions, for example ways of organising the supply systems of various necessities during World War II, and their spin-offs in the form of consulting firms which offered quantitative statistical and mathematical models for the construction of complex social systems. Another governmental commission which yielded similar effects occurred in the early days of America's cold-war relations with the Soviet Union, especially concerning the space programme.

Individuals of particular importance in this development included Frederick Taylor, who was the founding father of the scientific management movement in the early years of the twentieth century (which Barley and Kunda describe as the first business fad). Another whose work had a considerable impact was Elton Mayo, who during the 1930s was the protagonist of the human relations movement. Concerning the most prominent ideology which Barley and Kunda adjudge to have influenced the quality of organisational cultures, they single out Terrence Deal and Alan Kennedy (1982) and Tom Peters and Robert Waterman (1982), whose books sold millions worldwide.

The three studies briefly mentioned above have one thing in common, even though they stress different research questions. They all discuss the historical development of what McGill (1988) calls management myths, or managerial ideas as Huczynski (1993) prefers, or managerial ideologies according to Barley and Kunda (1992). In this regard the present study has a somewhat different focus. Here we start in the 1980s and attempt to study the diffusion of management books in Sweden, and scrutinise the production of a few significant works written by a few significant spokespersons. In this regard it is more in line with studies that discuss the popularity of management knowledge in terms of fashion. Abrahamson (1996) for instance, argues that there is an interchange between trendsetting organisations (such as consultants, business schools and business media) and fashion demand. All involved actors together constitute the trendsetting system. Although he is interested in trendsetters and how fashions travel he does not study the production of managerial manifestations in detail, which is done in the present study. Moreover, Røvik (1996) discusses the de-institutionalisation of institutionalised standards in terms of fashion. Here the focus is more on the use of management fads in local organisations. Although the consumption of fads is an important aspect of this study, it is not studied empirically in the present study. In the same vein as Abrahamson and Røvik is Kieser's (1997) study of management fashions where he explicitly notes the importance of myths and rhetoric for management concepts to reach the status of fashions. The rhetoric of popular books will be analysed in this study, but not in order to argue the fashionability of particular packages of management knowledge. Besides, the aim here is to analyse in detail the contents and production of a few selected management books. In the studies just referred to, the point has been more to discuss management fashions in general terms and develop theories for how the fashionability of management knowledge can be understood, not to examine in detail how popular management books are made.

To summarise, this section draws attention to the fact that few empirical studies have been made of either the popularity of managerial manifestations in general, or of the production and diffusion of management texts and knowledge. Earlier studies have applied either an historical or a critical approach to popular manifestations, focused on their development within academia. There have also been attempts to develop a theory of management fashions. The present study differs from these by focusing on their popularity as a modern phenomenon, the intention being to characterise, not criticise, popular management books to discern what they represent as elements in the organisational environment. Besides, we are concerned with popular, not academic management books. Thus the aim is to cover general tendencies concerning the origins of these popular books, and to identify some of the significant spokespersons in the field. Consequently it can be argued that the present study deals with a phenomenon of the organisational environment which has hitherto been neglected in the field of management studies. Therefore the empirical results of this study can be seen to complement those mentioned above. Thus an attempt is made to characterise what kind of environmental element popular managerial manifestations tend to represent, and how they may thereby be related to local organisational processes. In this regard a framework is developed which consists of studies chiefly made in the sociology of knowledge (e.g. Berger and Luckmann 1967; Whitley 1984a; Latour

1987) and in the new institutionalism in organisational analysis (e.g. DiMaggio and Powell 1991a; Scott and Meyer 1994). These approaches are explicitly discussed in Chapters 2 and 3. There we shall also explain how the present study may contribute to these traditions.

## The diffusion and production of management books[4]

This study seeks to perform detailed analyses of managerial texts. However, as the supply of management books is abundant it is not possible to study them all. In this respect texts which are widely distributed can be identified and their authors seen as more significant spokespersons of the general discourse than those who reach a smaller readership. In other words, due to their popularity, the authors of these books can be regarded as opinion leaders, fact builders (Latour 1987), or policy makers (DiMaggio and Powell 1983 [1991]), and their texts as significant voices in the general discourse. With this in mind, the diffusion of books is investigated in this study to enable the identification of significant spokespersons, followed by the selection of a few key texts in order to scrutinise their production. The selection of significant books is made here by considering the characteristics of the diffusion of books through different distribution channels, such as the stock in libraries, the supply of management book clubs, bestseller lists in business magazines, and books used in teaching at universities and business schools. In this way we can discern the general characteristics of the origin of such books. Thereafter, by focusing on a more specific selection of books, a few significant spokespersons who represent characteristics both on the general level and in the narrower populations can be identified. To discern the significance of these persons, patterns in the different distribution channels will be interpreted. In so doing the ambition is not to single out the most significant voices in the general managerial discourse, but rather to identify a few spokespersons who represent significant characteristics of the diffusion of management books. Following this, a selection of books written by these spokespersons can be selected for more detailed analyses of content and production process.

When the analysis moves to the production side, two strategies suggested by Latour (1987) in his study of science in action in technical laboratories, are employed. Here he argues that it is possible to reopen black boxes and see what is behind their surface. One strategy is to enter the text and analyse its content and rhetoric to see what is built into it, in other words its hidden agenda (55); the other strategy is to enter the context where it is produced, or in Latour's words, to 'sneak into the places where the papers are written and to follow the construction of facts in their most intimate details' (63). By so doing we can study the motives, considerations and social forces surrounding the creation and diffusion of managerial texts. Thus two major methods of studying the contents and production of management books will be employed: first, to enter the text; and second, to enter the context in which a text is created. This makes it possible to draw conclusions about what they represent as elements in the organisational environment. The text, i.e. the content, will be studied in three steps. One characterises it in terms of its background, its main issues and its rhetorical characteristics (i.e. its 'surface'). The second deconstructs the text into patterns of key discussions; and the third defines what the text represents as an environmental element in terms of knowledge or ideology. For studying the process of a text's production, the context in which it is produced can be entered through either ethnographic participating observations, or if an historical process is at issue, by conducting interviews with participants in the process and examining other texts and documents produced in the same context. In both cases, patterns can be sought which can later be discussed in relation to other studies of similar phenomena. The context in focus here is historical, which means that the latter strategy is applied. To this end, an analytical scheme will be applied consisting of four dimensions of the creation of managerial manifestation (research orientation, business orientation, concentration, standardisation).

This approach is close to what Wilson (1983) and McCloskey (1986) mean with their suggestion of an anti-methodology. Using Latour's (1987) terms the object is scrutinised from the outside, that is, by applying other methods than those used in the original text. It is thereby possible to study how texts, and thereby managerial manifestations, are produced.[5]

A pragmatic, step-by-step approach to the research object is applied here, since there are few prototype studies in the field of management studies to build upon. It would not be fair to call this study an ethnography, but the methodology employed is inspired by ethnography insofar as research objects are observed in order to interpret possible patterns. This approach suggests that the first step to take would be to map the field in focus. For this reason the first step taken here will be to search for patterns within the general managerial discourse: namely to study the supply of popular management books. For this reason we shall start by drawing up a map of the bibliographic field and selecting a few significant spokespersons before studying the production of popular texts in more detail.

However, before we can do this, the three core components of the model introduced in this chapter need to be more thoroughly discussed. By the same token we also need to discuss in further detail how the general managerial discourse and popular management books can be understood as elements of the organisational environment. This will now be further outlined, and the structure of the book briefly introduced.

## An outline of the study

Before we examine the points introduced above, it seems appropriate to present the agenda for the discussions to come.

In Chapter 2 an attempt is made to argue how the general managerial discourse may be related to organisations. In particular the elements of the model (Figure 1.1) – the general managerial discourse and the institutional environments of organisations – are described in more detail. In other words, a frame is presented here where empirical observations of the production and diffusion of popular management books are related to an institutional approach of the consumption thereof in organisations, and the connections between organisations and their environments. Chapter 3 gives a detailed discussion of the social constructive approach applied in this study to the complexities of the production and diffusion of management knowledge. It is argued that managerial manifestations can be moved in time and space, but that their contents are subject to interpretation and translation wherever they go.

Chapter 4 presents empirical observations of the supply of management books. An attempt is made to trace the origin of the predominant perspective in Swedish managerial discourse by examining the stock of books in libraries, books supplied by management book clubs, books on a bestseller list published in a business journal, sales statistics, and literature used in courses on management at Swedish universities and university colleges. Finally, a few significant spokespersons (or voices) in the Swedish managerial discourse are identified (Richard Normann; Tom Peters and Robert Waterman). In Chapter 5 two management books (*Service Management* and *In Search of Excellence*) written by the significant spokespersons identified in Chapter 4 are entered and a detailed analysis is made of their main messages, their rhetoric, their hidden agenda, and finally what they represent as elements of the organisational environment in terms of knowledge and ideology. In

Chapter 6 we enter the context (a consulting firm) in which one of these books (*Service Management*) was created. Here the aim is to go a step further than Chapter 5 and analyse the production process behind the book. Explicit attention is paid to the development of the context in which it was created. The discussion concentrates on the important motives, considerations and social forces which characterise this context.

In conclusion, in Chapter 7 the empirical findings are summarised and discussed in relation to the theoretical frame developed in Chapters 2 and 3. In particular we shall examine what popular management books (as representations of popular managerial discourse) contain, and what they thereby seem to represent as elements of the organisational environment. Moreover, with the conclusions from earlier phases of the analysis in mind, we shall here discuss what popular management books may mean for organisations when they are consumed therein.

Finally, in the Appendix, I present a detailed discussion of the methodological considerations behind the design of this study. Methods of analysing characteristics of the production and supply of popular management books are also developed and discussed in detail.

# 2 The managerial discourse and the organisational environment

## Introduction

In this chapter I shall first attempt to define what is meant by the concept of managerial discourse when used further on in this book. I shall then discuss how the general managerial discourse can be understood as an element in the complex relations between organisations and their environments. The managerial discourse is here regarded as an important aspect of the organisational environment which is often neglected in organisation-environment studies. Thus it is argued that if we would comprehend how organisations work, then we must also understand the discourse as something that is ongoing within and between organisations and societies. It is a discussion that goes beyond single organisations, organisational fields and societies. Seen in this way we need to understand what the discourse, and manifestations that represent dominant perspectives in the discourse, may mean for organisations.

This discussion was introduced briefly in Chapter 1, where a model of the design (Figure 1.1) of this study was developed. In this model, the general managerial discourse was described as consisting of presumptive interlinkage of the production, diffusion and consumption of managerial manifestations. The discourse, in turn, was related to the institutional environments of organisations, and organisational environments in general. In this chapter we shall discuss in more detail the relations between two of the core concepts of the model, namely the relations between the general managerial discourse, the environments of organisations, and organisations. The chapter starts with a discussion of the general managerial discourse, which is followed by a discussion of the organisational environment and how discourses can be understood as elements therein, and what this may mean for organisations.

## The general managerial discourse

The general managerial discourse is a core concept in this study. Its meaning may, however, seem diffuse. It is used here to label the phenomenon that consists of a great supply of various forms of manifestation of how organisations and management work. Since all these manifestations express opinions about management and organisations, it is not a neutral stock of textualised opinions. It is more appropriate to see them as contributions to an ongoing global debate about organisations and management. One interesting characteristic of this debate is that a large part of it takes place outside organisations. Participators in this discourse make their contributions when they textualise their ideas into speeches, seminars, teaching or articles and books. By so doing they make their textualisations more or less generally available. Almost everybody can access a book or a magazine. Seminars and speeches are more exclusive although they can be repeated to different audiences. Thus there is a difference between various kinds of manifestation in terms of how they are consumed. Some are consumed at the same moment as they are delivered, like speeches, seminars and lectures; whereas articles and books can be consumed over a longer period of time, and the consumption can be repeated. This also implies that they can be delivered but not consumed, i.e. they can reach a potential consumer who can then choose to delay consumption or not to consume at all. Nevertheless, as books or articles they have a capacity to reach a wider audience since they can be moved physically in time and space.

The effects of the consumption of a manifestation can differ. It may happen, for instance, that a seminar or a speech that is consumed 'in the moment of truth' has a greater impact than a book which does not vanish after it has been consumed. Hence the impact of a message on the receiver is connected to how they experience the message. This means that the rhetoric in which the message is clothed is of importance. Rhetoric means in this regard not only how the message is put in to words, but also the circumstances of its presentation. A speech or a seminar can be held in a glamorous atmosphere and delivered seductively by a brilliant speaker, while a book can be delivered in a brown paper parcel together with a lot of other important mail that must be dealt with urgently. Still, both these kinds of manifestations are delivered to organisations from actors in the environment, actors who produce ideas and package them into different forms such as speeches or books. Thus the label 'general managerial discourse' can be used when we talk about the aggregate of written and oral textualisations of the world of organisational and managerial life.

This is a quite wide definition of a discourse. More commonly perhaps, discourse is defined as an established mode of talking about certain issues in the world, or according to McCloskey (1986: 24–9), institutionalised forms of conversation. When we talk about the aggregate supply of managerial manifestations in the world, the concept of a general managerial discourse is useful. However, within this wide discourse there are several forms of conversation that are established in different social networks. In other words, particular social networks tend to have institutionalised language codes and rhetoric which are seen as the legitimate way to converse therein. A more explicit definition states that such discourses are less general, and involve institutionalised language codes for articulation of what in a particular setting is accepted as constituting credible representations of reality and events; in other words, patterns of ways to talk and act.

The concept of general managerial discourse is used in this study to denote an accumulated macro-conversation in the world on organisational and managerial life, which takes place both orally and in writing directly or indirectly between people, organisations and societies. As illustrated in Figure 1.1, this general conversation takes place within organisational environments, which means that manifestations within the discourse become elements of these environments. If by 'conversation' we mean two or more individuals who debate something face-to-face, the general discourse is not a conversation. But it can be seen as such on another level, since there is always someone, somewhere, writing and talking about management and leadership in the modern global community. Every single textualisation thereby becomes a contribution to the general discourse. Thus the general managerial discourse consists of all written and oral manifestations about management made by people through different kinds of action. Nevertheless, the general discourse does not consist of uniform manifestations in terms of content or rhetoric. In fact we can list six general categories of conversation:

1  teachers and researchers at business schools and universities
2  management gurus and others who hold executive seminars and write management books and articles in business magazines

3    management consultants who diagnose organisations' problems and give advice on how the problems should be solved
4    practitioners who interact in business and social relationships
5    politicians who promote policies concerning, for example, taxation of firms; who make rules about customs, and justify laws relating to job security or environmental issues
6    professional, interest and trade associations who guard the interests of different groups in, for example, macro-policy decisions and the setting of formal rules for foreign trade.

The form of conversation about managerial and organisational issues among these different categories of actors differs, since they communicate through different streams of institutionalised rhetoric. These streams can be seen as part-discourses within the general discourse. Four major part-discourses (i.e. four major institutionalised sets of rhetoric) can be identified: the popular, the academic, the practical and the political-managerial discourse.[1]

In each of the part-discourses there are particular actions which can be identified. The popular managerial discourse includes actions like journalism, consulting, practically oriented writing and external management development programmes. This discourse can be called popular since the manifestations therein are widely distributed and reach many people in different places. For instance, books sometimes become bestsellers, and journalistic manifestations can sometimes reach almost a entire population (in particular via TV). Another characteristic is that the manifestations often are directed to a lay public interested in managerial issues, which means that they tend to be popularised according to rhetorical codes that are believed to attract people in general and practitioners in organisations in particular. However, we are not really concerned with the layman's rhetoric here, since the popular managerial discourse is not that commonplace. Instead manifestations are likely to incorporate specific concepts such as bench-marking, business process re-engineering, total quality management, strategic planning, corporate culture, etc.

The most obvious actors are management gurus and consultants who write books and articles, who teach in management development programmes, and who diagnose problems in organisations and give advice on how to cure them. Other typical actors in this field are business journalists who hold interviews with people involved in business and who produce reports for radio, TV, newspapers and magazines. It also happens that journalists write biographies of famous businesspersons and managers. However, academics and practitioners may also pursue activities which belong in this field. For instance, it is not unusual for them to act as consultants outside of their strictly academic work, or to write books and articles which become popular.

The academic managerial discourse includes actions like academic research, academic writing, and teaching. Above all, the discourse concerns higher education and incorporates activities which are mainly pursued by academics who teach, conduct research and write academic books and articles on management. However, the main reason for speaking of a specific academic discourse is that the rhetorical codes are of a particular kind. Thus, to be accepted as an authoritative voice, the scholar is likely to use a specific academic jargon based on references (sometimes specific works) and systematism (cf. Latour 1987; McCloskey 1986). In this respect the academic discourse is extreme in regard to the others since they all are more commonplace.

The political-managerial discourse includes such actions as enacting legislation, devising political programmes, making political speeches and writing articles for the mass media. The main actors are politicians and political experts who sometimes, like the actors from the other fields, produce articles and books on management-related issues, but their crucial importance in the development of the managerial discourse is probably that they produce laws and regulations for how business may be practised. Parts of this discourse, i.e. when it concerns legislation, are specific. In this regard the conversation codes can be defined as juridical. With respect to political programmes and speeches, the rhetoric is more commonplace but draws mainly upon particular political ideologies which give it a certain character.

Finally, the practical managerial discourse consists of practitioners' internal management development programmes, social interaction, practical actions, personal and social experiences and the activities of trade, interest and professional organisations. The major actors are practitioners who interact with colleagues and discuss management-related problems with them (but also with their friends). In practice, communication sometimes involves written internal documents and speeches given by the management on various occasions, both formal and informal. However, the crucial way whereby ideas are developed and diffused is probably through practical experience in practising management. In addition, professional and trade associations are probably important voices since they are actually commissioned to work as voices in the political debate in society at large.

The practical discourse can be differentiated from the others since practitioners, when they discuss management issues, often depart from experienced problems which they need to solve in one way or another.

It happens, of course, that they converse on management in other situations as well, but are more likely than academics, consultants, journalists or politicians to use communication codes which are more directly connected to practical problems which they have faced or believe they will face in the future. In this regard, non-practitioners who discuss management-related problems in organisations are more likely to discuss the principles of management and leadership rather than the sharp end of practice.

Through manifestations of management that can be defined as actions which can be placed in these four major part-discourses, the contents thereof are communicated and diffused between organisations and societies. This means that ideas, norms and models of organisational identity, structure and actions are carried by discourse in time and space. The borders between the part-discourses are indefinite and interlinked, but they are also linked to various other social discourses (cf. Foucault 1971; 1993).

Note that when distinguishing between different part-discourses we are talking here about actions, not actors. For instance, it is not uncommon for one person to participate in several discourses, since it can happen that popular books are written by academics who normally pursue serious research and who teach at universities. It is also common for them to accept consultancy assignments and participate in management development programmes. Similarly, consultants may teach at universities, write academic texts and carry out research, at the same time as they produce popular books and articles and are involved in management training. Practitioners might also write popular books and articles, but are also sometimes involved in teaching at universities. Politicians are probably most likely to work with politics when it concerns management issues, but they occasionally commission academics, consultants and practitioners to participate in investigations and write particular reports. Furthermore, many consultants, practitioners and politicians have qualifications from universities and business schools where they have attended classes in management. So there is a complex interaction between these part-discourses, but they have specific requisites which distinguish them from each other. Popular books are, however, seen as intermediaries between the part-discourses, or rather as carriers of knowledge, myths, beliefs, institutions and ideologies between them. In fact, popular management books which are widely distributed can be perceived as significant voices in the general conversation. This means that there also are reasons to believe that they reflect common formulations of management and leadership by many voices, irrespective of whether they are academics, consultants, practitioners or politicians. Hence they are perceived as important 'voices' in the general managerial discourse in society, inasmuch as due to their wide diffusion they can be considered essential for the institutionalisation of general norms, expectations and professional standards of management in the modern western world. This also makes them significant elements of the environments of organisations.

In the next section we will elaborate on how the discourse can be understood as a layer in the organisational environment, its manifestations understood as elements therein, and how all this is likely to have impact on organisations.

## Environments and organisations

The relations between elements in organisations' global environments and local processes are not only very complex and difficult to illustrate, they are also difficult to fully understand. Therefore it is not easy to claim that a particular manifestation represents causal relations of how tendencies in the general environments of organisations are textualised and thereby become elements in the general managerial discourse. Furthermore, we can also question the assumption that manifestations of managerial life are diffused to practitioners who are thereby induced to change their behaviour. Hence, if we take the complexity of the world seriously, it is instead more relevant to take a position where all environmental elements are considered to be simultaneously and continuously at work. Thus organisational processes are always current, as are oral or written textualisations of what they do. This means that textualisations of managerial and organisational life, based on observations and experiences from historical organisational processes, are in production, at the same time as new processes are in progress. The spread of ideas can therefore be understood as being facilitated not solely by means of textualisations in books or activities taken by management consultants. In fact there are several complex routes ideas take when they move in time and space. As argued above, the general managerial discourse can be seen as an aggregate of all forms of textualisations of management over time. Here we will argue that organisational processes are embedded in this discourse, as they are in so many other dimensions, systems and elements. Thus the general managerial discourse is only one layer of the organisational environment; yet it is a part that has so far been neglected in studies of this environment.

The relationship between elements of the organisational environment and local organisational processes is not a new field of interest. In fact it is a major theme in a vast number of studies; as Meyer (1994) points out, probably because every aspect of organisational life is affected by environment. This may be self-evident, but Meyer implies that in the global society there are environmental elements that are often neglected, such as dominant rules and ideologies. Moreover, such elements are not natural, i.e. they do not exist by themselves, but are produced and maintained by organisations and professions, in systems such as education, research and consultation. Thus do the activities of such people contribute to the structuring of the organisational environment. The structured environment then impinges on what is happening in organisations. If we would better understand organisational processes we also need to take these aspects of the environment into account, though they may seem abstract and are often neglected.

However, relations between organisations and environments have long been important topics among students of organisations. Before trying to define where in the environment the general managerial discourse belongs, it might therefore be appropriate to recall how relations between organisations and their environments are discussed elsewhere. The most commonly cited works are probably Burns and Stalker (1961), Woodward (1965), Lawrence and Lorsch (1967), Thompson (1967) and Galbraith (1973). They mainly see the environment as a given, to which organisations have to adapt their structure, and consider that different industries have certain antecedents which should be met by certain organisational structures, if organisations want to be successful and survive. The perspective advocated in these studies dominated the field in the 1970s, but these scholars were chiefly concerned with technical features of environments, and disregarded the institutional elements (Scott and Meyer 1983; 1991). It has been argued that these studies underestimated the extent to which organisations are connected to, and affected by larger systems of relations which go beyond the observable technical ones (*ibid.*). Consequently Scott and Meyer state that organisational processes must be understood as embedded in larger systems of relations where beliefs, myths and ideologies in the wider society and in local social networks, side-by-side with technical relations, are founding elements. The same point is made by Meyer and Rowan (1977; 1991), who also call attention to what they define as symbolic elements of the organisational environment, such as institutionalised beliefs, rules and roles. Furthermore, Scott (1991) emphasises that organisational environments not only consist of elements and relations directly involved when products or services are exchanged and produced; they also comprise cultural and symbolic elements. Thus, following Scott and Meyer (1983; 1991), this implies that elements in the organisational environment can be divided into two categories: the technical and the institutional.

Scott and Meyer define technical environments as delimited by the time and place where production and exchange of products or services occurs in a market. Organisations active in such environments focus on efficiency in their production systems. This is because they are 'rewarded' for effectiveness of production. In such environments organisations concentrate their efforts on controlling and coordinating their technical processes. They try to buffer or protect the technical core from disturbances in the environment (cf. Thompson 1967).

However, the organisational environment does not end in technical aspects, since these in their turn can be seen as embedded in institutional environments (Scott and Meyer 1983; 1991). These can be described as formal rules imposed by governments and trade associations, but also by informal requirements to which individual organisations must conform if they are to receive support and legitimacy. Such requirements may stem from different sources, e.g. regulatory bodies authorised by the state, professional or trade associations, or generalised belief systems which impose rules of conduct for specific types of organisation (cf. Meyer and Rowan 1977; 1991; Meyer 1994). It is a mark of organisational operations in institutional environments that they are 'rewarded' according to how they conform to institutionalised requirements and beliefs.

However, even though Scott and Meyer divide environments into technical and institutional parts, they do not insist that these are mutually exclusive states. They hold that the two coexist and that organisations are embedded in systems of relations of both kinds. A similar argument is presented by DiMaggio and Powell (1983 [1991]) who introduce the term 'organisational field', which they define as 'organizations that, in the aggregate constitute a recognized area of institutional life: key suppliers, resource and product consumers, regulatory agencies, and other organizations which produce similar services or products' (1991: 64–5). They state that such fields emerge from processes of interaction among organisations, inter-organisational structures of domination and patterns of coalition, the information load with which organisations in a field must contend, and mutual awareness among participants in a set of organisations. It is characteristic of an organisational field that the participants are linked to each other in such a way that they are actually involved in a common, and often unconscious enterprise. Due to these linkages, DiMaggio and Powell argue, there are social forces which lead organisations to homogeneity of structure, culture and actions (*ibid.*: 64).

## Trends in the environment and carriers of managerial manifestations

Above it was argued that organisations can be seen as located in systems and fields regulated by both technical and institutional elements. This means that organisations can be seen as embedded in systems of ideologies, beliefs, myths, standards, norms, rules and regulations which tend to be worldwide, i.e. go beyond organisations, organisational fields and societies (e.g. Meyer 1994). In fact, the sum of all organisational relations in the world can be seen as an aggregated system which provides many models for organisation. Thus it is within this worldwide system where models of organisational order are constructed, spread and consumed.

Trends which appear on this level can be regarded as general global trends in the organisation and structuring of social order in modern society. In this regard they contribute to the institutionalisation of certain worldwide, universal patterns of behaviour, ideologies, and scientific doctrines, whatever their content. Strang and Meyer (1994) discuss one such trend when they argue that there is a global move towards an homogenisation of rules and ideologies in modern society, which is mainly based on a search for 'rationality' (i.e. a tendency to structure relations in means-ends relationships). As a consequence, they argue, rules and ideologies of organisation and management tend to develop towards global, 'rationalised' standards. Such tendencies are often described as a struggle towards 'modernity' (cf. Clegg 1990; Giddens 1991).

The appearance of certain tendencies is one thing, but their construction and maintenance are something else. Although some tendencies have reached a high degree of institutionalisation, they do not exist as natural objects. Meyer (1994) argues, for instance, that their origin can regularly be traced back to organisational and professional systems (like the education system, professional and trade associations, political systems and management consultants) which function as 'rationalising agents' in the global society. Within these systems we find actors who do nothing else but in various ways tell organisations what to do (cf. Meyer 1996). In this way they provide organisations with ideas, models, standards, knowledge, ideologies, rules, directives and advice. In this way they rationalise the environment for organisations and provide the rationale for what an organisation is supposed to be and how it is supposed to work. Consequently, it is in these systems we can find the origins of environmental rationalisation. To locate the ultimate origin is, however, more or less impossible, since ideas are likely to occur at different levels of these relations, i.e. either in organisations' immediate social networks, in particular organisational fields, or in the society as a whole. This is why it is so difficult to talk in terms of the origin of an idea. Meyer argues, for instance that ideas are carried in worldwide systems of organisations and professions. As a consequence, he argues (*ibid.*: 31) 'new and elaborated models of management, accounting, consulting or personnel administration pop up almost everywhere, in trends or waves of a general character' (see also Brunsson 1997). However, although this explanation is reasonable, the importance for the spread of certain ideas to particular organisations or organisational fields via specific actors like certain management gurus or consultants, cannot be ignored. Perhaps the importance of specific actors in this regard is primarily on the local level, where they contribute to the transportation of an idea into certain organisations. Whether or not an idea can be traced back to its origin, organisations are embedded in these different levels of systems which impinge on their identity, structure and activities. Specific actors play an important role here by regularly keeping organisations in direct contact with institutionalised elements in the environment. Although it is difficult to trace the ultimate origin of such elements, this does not mean that they have been created from a *tabula rasa*, i.e. they are not produced, diffused and consumed in a vacuum. This means that one single actor can hardly be seen as the creator of an idea. Instead it is more appropriate to see single actors as parts of a system, and that they articulate and carry ideas already constructed or under construction in the system. Perhaps it is appropriate to say that these actors produce manifestations of management that they carry between organisations and societies, but hardly that they create completely new ideas. Such processes rather take place within a context of wider relations (Meyer 1994).

In the next section we shall elaborate on the general managerial discourse as a layer in the organisational environment where organisational and managerial life are textualised and as such carried between places. This has hitherto not been discussed explicitly in the new institutionalism. DiMaggio and Powell (1991b) call, however, for studies which consider links between macro (general) phenomena and micro (local) processes from a new institutional perspective. As argued here, the general managerial discourse can be seen as such a link insofar as it mainly consists of local stories that are de-contextualised and then brought back to different local contexts.

## The general managerial discourse as a layer in the institutional environment of organisations

Following the above  argument, it seems most appropriate to see the kind of conversation that popular books represent as a layer of an organisation's institutional environment. This is, however, a form of conversation that does not take place between two individuals, and is not directly and physically related to the production and exchange of products or services on markets. It is instead an indirect form of conversation in which we all in one way or another are involved when we, in various ways, vocally or in documents, textualise organisational and managerial life. Thereby we all participate in the social processes where knowledge, myths, ideas and ideologies are created and diffused throughout society. This means that beliefs of management and organisations are formed in the discourse, but also that ideas, by being textualised, gain a capacity to travel between organisations and societies. To be more precise, the general discourse can be defined as a layer that consists of textualised cultural elements of an organisation's institutional environment. In a way it can also be seen as a bank of textualisations of organisational and managerial life. In this way, popular books and other forms of managerial manifestations can be seen as 'withdrawals' from this world bank. Popular books can travel far and reach many people; they have the capacity to appear almost anywhere – in teaching at universities, in different kinds of public and private organisation, as references in political life, and in discussions amongst the general public. Thus popular books carry representations of managerial and organisational life to several social networks in modern society, and can thereby be seen as intermediaries of representations between not only organisations, but also organisational fields and societies. Nevertheless, whether or not a single popular management book has any influence on local organisational processes can be questioned. However, here they are seen as voices in the general discourse, which means that they become representations of a general phenomenon in the organisational environment. In this regard, we instead discuss the relation between a general environmental phenomenon and organisations. For instance, if popular books are textualisations and carriers of dominant perspectives in the general discourse, then it can be argued that the interesting relation is not between one book and one organisational process, but between the general popular discourse and the organisation. Only when books are seen from this perspective is there a point in discussing how they may impinge on organisations.

Nevertheless, before we can examine the possible relationship between a general discourse and local organisational processes in more detail, we need to determine what kind of environmental element it is. This far we have stated that the general managerial discourse is a layer consisting of textualised cultural elements mainly belonging to the institutional environment. Below we shall attempt to localise the general managerial discourse in this environmental layer.

## *Institutional pressure, discourses and organisations*

The impact on organisations from elements in the institutional environment has been an important issue in the new institutional organisational analysis for a long time. In DiMaggio and Powell's seminal study (1983 [1991]) this kind of influence is referred to as an institutional pressure on organisations. They identify three institutional mechanisms and argue that the pressure from the environment caused by these mechanisms forces organisations operating in the same organisational field to be homogeneous. The mechanisms they introduce are coercive, mimetic, and normative isomorphic pressure. Each mechanism has certain antecedents, and it can be argued that the general discourse is a source for all of them. Let us, however, first recall what DiMaggio and Powell mean, and then discuss in what way the general managerial discourse may be involved here.

Coercive isomorphic pressure is described as the social forces related to political influence and the problem of legitimacy. It results from a coercive pressure in society which is exerted on organisations by others upon which they are dependent in various ways; e.g. rules and regulations developed by governments and different trade associations. This kind of pressure is usually formalised and controlled by national and international governmental organisations. In this way the state obliges organisations to do certain things in a certain way. If they break the regulation the state may punish them by, for example, sending those who are in charge to jail or levying a fine on the organisation. This kind of coercive pressure is formal and is, due to its legal nature, a powerful mechanism for creating isomorphism among organisations. This pressure is not only national. In the last decade we have seen a growing tendency towards transnational regulation. One example of this is the establishment of the European Union, where a major project is to harmonise national regulations with EU regulations; and another example is the establishment of the World Trade Organisation (WTO) whose task is to regulate international trade. Although these organisations are products of the 1990s, this does not mean that there were no transnational regulations before this. Rather, their establishment indicates that transnational regulation has become more important.

Mimetic isomorphic pressure is another kind of mechanism which, according to DiMaggio and Powell, is directed towards imitation enforced by uncertainty. This means that organisations are not forced to act like others; they choose of their own accord to imitate other organisations. The trigger for such homogenisation is that when organisations and organisational members experience uncertainty, they may model themselves on other organisations in order to reduce this enacted uncertainty. This pressure differs from the coercive insofar as organisations imitate role models by their own free will. Organisations around the world seek uncertainty reduction and legitimacy by imitating a relatively small set of popular organisational and management models. Such models can be imitated unintentionally, indirectly through employee transfer or turnover, or through activities taken by other organisations such as consulting firms or industry trade associations working specifically with the transportation of management models. DiMaggio and Powell argue that in order to be accepted by other parties concerned and thus obtain legitimacy for opinions or rights to make decisions, they use well known environmental models to devise their own concepts and perform actions interpreted as correct. Or as DiMaggio and Powell put it (1983; 1991: 70):

> New organisations are modelled upon old ones throughout the economy, and managers actively seek models upon which to build (Kimberly 1980). ... Large organisations choose from a relatively small set of major consulting firms, which, like Johnny Appleseeds, spread a few organisational models throughout the land.

Consequently what influential elements in the environment – the so-called policy makers – say, believe, think, and do is crucial. It is therefore important to increase our understanding of what they do by, for instance, observing how they talk, the rules they make and the standards of successful behaviour which they represent, as well as how and when they formulate norms and opinions. By virtue of their positions or roles, these policy makers express, and represent, schedules or maps of the concepts institutionalised in the field or in society at large. As a result, especially if they are widely disseminated, there is little variation in the legitimate models of organisational structure available for selection, since many organisations tend to model themselves on similar organisations in their field whom they perceive to be more legitimate or successful.

DiMaggio and Powell's third mechanism, normative isomorphism, is also voluntary by definition. It stems primarily from professionalisation in the sense of intentions to control the 'production of producers' (Larson 1977: 49–52) by the collective efforts of practitioners to define conditions, methods, and a cognitive base and authorisation of the autonomy of occupational work. In this regard, especially in long-established professions such as medicine, accounting and the law, the professional norms and ethics are coercive insofar as you can lose your authority to act as a professional in your field if you break the professional rules. However, in younger and less institutionalised professions (such as management consultancy, stockbroking, and temporary employment – 'temping') the professional rules are much less rigid and there is no central authority that can punish or ban anyone from acting as professionals in their respective fields. In this regard two aspects of professionalisation can be mentioned. One comprises the formal education and the cognitive base associated with certain universities which give legitimacy to people with similar experiences and cognitive base. The other consists of growing professional networks spanning organisations, in which new models diffuse rapidly. Managers and management consultants are an extreme example of the latter category. There are networks where management and management consulting are seen as professions. This suggests that professional managers could practise their professional management in any organisation irrespective of national, local or industrial logic. It also suggests that management consulting is a profession with certain requirements. Norms for professionalism in different areas are developed in different arenas such as universities, institutes for professional training, and professional and trade associations. This means that within specific social networks there are forces for homogenising standards. Such standards are, however, not only developed for professions. They occur more or less consciously in many areas. They can also take different forms. For example, it is routine for many companies only to recruit potential executives with degrees from certain universities or colleges. Another form of normative rule stems from the recent development of industrial, national, European and international standards of more or less formal characters. Examples in this regard are TQM (Total Quality Management), ISO 9000 and

EQA (the European Quality Award). These are three forms of standards that have the same roots and they suggest the same organisational model, i.e. an organisation where quality in all processes is guaranteed and where the notion of constant improvement rules. Thus the existence and growing importance of this kind of organisation since the mid-1980s is a normative pressure on organisations to adjust their forms and processes to international standards. This pressure is somewhat different from the tendencies of professionalisation in both older and younger professions, but still, it is a force towards normalisation among actors, i.e. it encourages them to normalise their activities according to internationally established standards.

There are regulations such as formal rules and laws that by definition are coercive. However, coerciveness and its antithesis, voluntarism, are complex concepts. Especially when informal regulation caused by mimetic and normative mechanisms are considered. This complexity is underlined when we consider another kind of pressure on organisations suggested by Scott (1995). He discusses cognitive environmental elements, by which he means that organisations are forced to become more homogeneous by a cognitive pressure from the environment. This concept does not challenge the mechanisms discussed above, it is more to be seen as another way to conceptualise the elements and pressures on the organisational environment. Scott's argument is that there are institutionalised categories and types in the environment that force social entities to conform to them. One example in this regard is the current trend of organising, i.e. the construction of organisations (Brunsson and Sahlin-Andersson 1998). This means that more and more social entities conform to the rationale of organisation, that is, they present themselves and attempt to structure their activities in terms of identity, hierarchy and rationality. Such pressure is not formal, although it can be experienced as coercive. By definition it is voluntary to choose whether or not one likes to look upon certain activities as organised according to the organisation rationale. In practice, however, this might very well be experienced as a coercive pressure. Other examples in this regard are typifications of what a manager is and categorisations of characteristics of good and bad managers: very few managers are likely to aspire to what is not generally considered good leadership practice. These cognitive environmental elements are, in contrast to national and transnational formal regulation, not controlled by a central authority with the power to punish social groups or leaders if they refuse to follow the trend, but actors will nevertheless be punished by the system if they risk not being regarded as legitimate and modern. As a result, because of cognitive elements in different fields, there is a pressure on organisations to be increasingly homogeneous and organised around particular rituals which conform to wider institutions, based on rules and expectations in and beyond explicit organisational fields.

To conclude, management books can be defined as carrying representations of management and organisation. These can be characterised as accounts representing either knowledge, ideology, myths, beliefs or institutions. Irrespective of the manner in which they can be characterised, they provide ideas for the reproduction of particular forms of social order. Since some books are distributed widely, it can be argued that such texts may not contribute to different isomorphic mechanisms among organisations in the same organisational field, but also between fields and societies (cf. Meyer 1994). For instance, books can be regarded as elements of cognitive isomorphism, since they contribute to the creation and maintenance of cognitive social categories and typifications. If homogeneous accounts of organisational and managerial life are distributed in books to a worldwide public, they may trigger a general institutionalisation of these accounts. They can also indirectly contribute to coercive isomorphism, since some voices (such as popular books or management consulting firms) that attain great popularity thereby contribute to the creation and preservation of both formal rules and informal cultural expectations. In other words, by being articulated, circulated and perhaps repeated in general conversations about management and leadership, popular ideologies, myths or institutions in modern society may be applied when laws, regulations and cultural expectations are created, since they articulate norms and notions of good and bad managerial and organisational behaviour. Popular managerial texts might also trigger mimetic isomorphism in the sense that they articulate models of organisational and managerial life which are said to have been applied in successful companies. In this regard such models might appeal to people's uncertainty, and thereby be adopted by many organisations as attractive solutions. Finally, popular texts may also encourage normative isomorphism insofar as they articulate and disseminate models of professional behaviour and articulate management standards.

To some extent, the general managerial discourse may promote these mechanisms when dominant voices in the discourse become elements of considerable importance in the construction of these forms of pressure. In particular, what in this chapter is called the popular managerial discourse is most likely to represent dominant voices in the general discourse due to the popularity and wide distribution of certain manifestations such as books.

## The general managerial discourse: where ideas are textualised

In this chapter it has been argued that the general managerial discourse can be seen as a layer of the institutional environment of an organisation, where cultural elements such as knowledge, ideologies or myths are articulated. It is by being textualised either orally or in written documents that ideas are given the capacity to travel between places and thereby become elements in the environments of different organisations. Although ideas can travel via the local history of organisations, through routines and symbols, it is by being textualised, i.e. manifested, that management ideas are enabled to travel long distances both in time and space. Thus the general managerial discourse represents a layer of the environment where the conversation about managerial issues is textualised and often de-contextualised. As argued here, this general discourse can be divided into four parts where different forms of conversation are carried out: the academic, the practical, the political, and the popular managerial discourse. This means that the general managerial discourse can be seen as something of a 'world bank' from which manifestations are withdrawn in order to be installed in different local settings. The most commonly withdrawn manifestations, i.e. representations of the popular managerial discourse, are likely to have the greatest impact on organisations. The discourse, in its different forms, impinges on institutional pressures on organisations from their environments, but the most widely distributed manifestations are believed to be of most importance. Through coercive, cognitive, mimetic and normative mechanisms in the environment, the pressure to which the popular managerial discourse in particular contributes, then influences the daily life of organisations.

So far so good; but although this method of locating the discourse in the organisational environment and attempting to describe how it affects organisations may seem reasonable, it does not tell us much of what happens when the manifestations meet local organisations. As suggested by the studies referred to above, the institutional mechanisms would make organisations more homogeneous worldwide. Thus it can be argued that elements that trigger isomorphic mechanisms of either coercive, cognitive, mimetic or normative pressure on organisations, are all textualised in the general managerial discourse. In this regard the general managerial discourse, and especially the dominant voices therein, may affect organisations via these mechanisms. However, as will be argued in the next chapter, the great diffusion of the same manifestations, and the existence of institutional pressures on organisations to do certain things, does not necessarily mean that organisations everywhere become homogeneous in their form and processes.

# 3 When management knowledge moves

## Introduction

In the previous chapter we learned that management ideas, once textualised, gain the capacity to move between places. It was also argued that the general managerial discourse represents an aggregate of all forms of manifestation. In this regard the general discourse can be seen as a layer in the organisational environment where ideas are articulated orally or in writing. It was also argued that it thereby impinges on the construction of the contents of different institutional environmental mechanisms, which in their turn are believed to affect what happens in local organisations. However, thus far we have not discussed what happens when managerial manifestations move in time and space, i.e. when they are de-contextualised from the setting where they are developed to become parts of other processes in other organisations and societies. Can they, for instance, be seen as black boxes that can be moved everywhere without risk of being reinterpreted, or do they become edited and translated in the process of their diffusion? In this chapter we shall attempt to develop a framework within which movements in time and space of management knowledge and managerial manifestations can be understood. In this regard we shift perspective and leave the macro level, namely the general managerial discourse, and focus on the manifestations and what is likely to happen as they are diffused. We will bring attention to the three remaining elements in the model for this study presented in Chapter 1 (Figure 1.1) that were not discussed in detail, namely: the production, diffusion and consumption of managerial manifestations.

Nevertheless, although the focus here is on managerial manifestations, a core concept in this chapter is management knowledge, since knowledge is what managerial manifestations often claims to represent. This means that we here draw a distinction between the meaning of management knowledge and managerial manifestations. For this reason we shall first discuss the complex and somewhat blurred meaning of knowledge in social science in general and in the field of management studies in particular. Next, we focus on the production of managerial manifestations, and then on the diffusion of management knowledge. In this regard the common view of the diffusion of knowledge is questioned, and the mobility in time and space of managerial manifestations is discussed in terms of translation processes.

## Knowledge in social science

The most common – but also the most idealistic – meaning is probably that knowledge is believed to represent undeniable facts and objective truths. Perhaps it is possible to achieve this status in laboratories within certain disciplines of the natural sciences such as physics, biology or chemistry, but the meaning of knowledge in social science is more ambiguous. It happens that the laborative ideal is imitated within social science; nevertheless, on the contrary, it also happens that knowledge is seen as socially constructed and consists of institutionalised beliefs. The attitudes to these issues are particularly important, since the definition of knowledge also has consequences for what we mean by its diffusion, production and consumption. For instance, some argue that 'knowledge' can be achieved through the application of standardised methodologies, and that its pure meaning can thereafter be communicated in a text. On the other hand, others hold that the meaning of knowledge is dependent on the social relativity of a representation of reality.

> What is 'real' to a Tibetan monk may not be 'real' to an American businessman.
>
> (Berger and Luckmann 1967: 15)

With this exemplification Berger and Luckmann seek to show that what is enacted as real varies between different contexts, since reality and the knowledge thereof are 'justified by the fact of their social relativity' (*ibid.*). They also argue that neither social reality nor knowledge are natural phenomena like, for example, forests, rivers, mountains and even technical and chemical artefacts which are composed of natural objects. Instead, as the simple example of the monk and the businessman shows, notions of reality in social patterns and events are socially constructed from processes of negotiation in particular contexts between individuals and collectives. Such processes result in a collective enactment of reality, and an enactment of knowledge of reality, i.e. what is believed to be 'real'. Sometimes such socially constructed subjects are so rigorously structured – i.e. well defined, well established and commonly used as representations of particular events – that they are regarded in some contexts as if they actually were natural objects, i.e. that they have become institutions embodied in routines which are taken for granted in the everyday life of a particular group of individuals. In consequence, events in certain social networks will probably be judged on the basis of these enactments. When focusing on knowledge, this complexity means that what is accepted as knowledge concerns how this is related to what is considered as knowledge in particular social contexts. Consequently, neither reality nor knowledge has a single meaning which is valid in any context. For instance, there are probably differences between the views of reality held by religious fundamentalists and atheists, by managers and employees, by managers of public and private organisations, by managers of large and small organisations, and by managers in China, Turkey, France, Hungary, Russia and the US.

Berger and Luckmann say that 'the observable differs between societies in terms of what is taken for granted as "knowledge" in them' (*ibid.*). This means that there is a variety of assumptions of knowledge in the society, and consequently almost any body of knowledge can be socially established as representing 'reality' and 'knowledge' of 'reality'. The meanings of both knowledge and reality thereby become social constructions, not natural objects. In other words, conceptions of reality and knowledge are created through conscious and unconscious negotiations between different actors – i.e. in the process of the social construction of reality – where both formal and informal standards are created and maintained for judging whether or not something should be considered as 'knowledge' in this setting. Consequently, what is regarded as knowledge varies between different social networks.

The discussion above may seem difficult to follow. The significance of the argument may, however, be clarified by an example. Let us refer to Bruno Latour (1987: ch. 6) and his discussion of a similar dilemma in technoscience, where he uses the medieval seafarers as an example. They sailed to distant, unknown coasts. They were experienced sailors and knew how to handle the fury of the elements and how to navigate across open sea, but initially they did not know what the distant coastline looked like, particularly in comparison with the knowledge of it already possessed by its local inhabitants. However, having discovered these outlandish places, seafarers wrote down their observations and drew maps of the coastline. Once returned, they disseminated their experiences by showing the maps to others.

This leads to questions which indicate a number of important dilemmas in defining what knowledge is:

1   Is it possible to say that the seafarer who wrote the maps had knowledge of the coastline if we compare it with that of the local inhabitants?
2   Could later seafarers acquire knowledge about the field by reading the maps drawn by the early adventurers?
3   Can the later seafarer's kind of knowing be compared with the kind of knowing the inhabitants have?
4   Who does really know? The inhabitants, for whom the coastline and everything associated with it is everyday routine? The seafarers, who acquired their knowledge by experience and observations over a limited period of time? Or those who sit in their armchairs at home and read the maps drawn by the early adventurers?
5   What are the characteristics of the seafarers' and of the inhabitants' discourse about the coastline? It may well be that the inhabitants' arguments for avoiding dangerous waters are founded on associations with supernatural beings, or commonsense attitudes taken for granted by all, while the seafarers' reasons are based on natural observations and then de-contexualised and represented by lines and dots on a map.

Following from this it can be argued that the social relativity of an argument is crucial. The point in the example here is to avoid the dangerous waters. The best way to make people avoid them might be to pursue the institutionalised discourse relevant to that particular setting. Otherwise it might happen that people do not understand what the argument represents, namely to stay away from dangerous waters.

We are here speaking of a natural phenomenon (the coastline) which *per se* has a natural constitution that is objectively true (land, water, islands, bays, rocks) and where it is a fact that particular spots are dangerous and unhealthy for a person to approach. Nevertheless, we are also discussing ways of representing this natural feature, through supernatural legends or through an 'objective' chart. The complexity of acquiring knowledge is also implied. It can either happen by listening to 'superstitious' stories, by trial and error, or by consulting the map. Concerning the complexity of acquiring 'knowledge', Latour (1987: 219) writes:

> The first time we encounter some event, we do not know it; we start knowing something when it is at least the second time we encounter it, which is when it is familiar to us.

Consequently, a foreigner or a newcomer to a field will always lack knowledge; especially if by 'knowledge' we mean 'familiarity with events, places and people seen many times over' (*ibid.*: 220). However, if it is possible to reproduce relevant information about a situation – or find means of transferring experiences from one situation to another (for instance in the form of a map) – so that the foreigner can 'see' the situation for the first time without being there in person, then we can say that this way of depicting the circumstances can be defined as knowledge. The reason is that if the newcomer can travel in territory represented by a map (or a legend) through having seen the map or heard the story, then they have been able to acquire relevant 'knowledge' in this context. Thus knowledge can be diffused through completely different discourses; one which is based on what can be called technical rhetoric (the map) and another based on what can be called superstitious rhetoric (the legend).

Consequently it seems that relevant 'knowledge' required to handle new situations can be gained in different ways. This again is discussed by Latour, who maintains that we cannot understand what knowledge is if we do not understand what gaining knowledge means. He writes:

> As we see, what is called 'knowledge' cannot be defined without understanding what gaining knowledge means. In other words, 'knowledge' is not something that could be described by itself or by opposition to 'ignorance' or to 'belief', but only by considering a whole cycle of accumulation: how to bring things back to a place for someone to see it for the first time so that others might be sent again to bring other things back.
>
> (Latour 1987: 220)

So, according to Latour, if a representation of 'reality' is to be called knowledge, it must be

1   mobile in order to be properly represented so that it can be transmitted to other persons;

2    stable so that the represented manifestation can be moved between specific social networks without losing its relevance; and further, it must be

3    combinable in order to be accumulated, aggregated or shuffled, no matter what its content (*ibid.*: 223).[1]

However, we must never forget that a representation of reality enacted as mobile, stable or combinable pertains to its social relativity in particular social networks (Berger and Luckmann 1967). Therefore there may be different assumptions in the society concerning whether or not something is to be seen as knowledge. Nevertheless, Latour's three 'requisites' constitute a general definition of the term 'knowledge'. Another question arises, however, if people with different backgrounds and experiences arrive at different interpretations of particular manifestations, since this concerns interpretations of the meaning of representations of reality. Latour's arguments can therefore be useful as a general definition of how representations which can be called 'knowledge' are 'organised', i.e. of their rhetorical characteristics. In particular this means how the author of a text communicates his or her considerations, references, systematic moves, etc., to enable the reader to follow the argument and its relevance to the comments of others. Such organisation of a text does not render it more 'true', but makes it mobile, since fundamental considerations are communicated. It also makes it stable, since the arguments are related to other discussions; and it becomes combinable, since it can be criticised on the grounds that some points have not been considered, or it can be further developed when used as point of departure to introduce more references, or related to similar discussions on other topics.

This definition is of course an ideal type, and in this sense extreme. Its opposite extremity is ideology, which thereby can be defined as texts built up on closed arguments in the sense that labels are used without being explained. Moreover, statements, platitudes and metaphors are likely to be used more or less frequently as rhetorical tools in order to persuade the reader of all the benefits of a text. Thus the more we find unelaborated myths, fashions, institutionalised beliefs, and a lack of references and openness in terms of methodological considerations, the more ideological the text.[2] But again, it is important to recognise that whether or not rhetoric can be defined as knowledge or ideology, this does not necessarily mean that knowledge equals truth and ideology non-truth. Another thing important to note here is that we talk about representations of something, and not the complete, true story about it.

## The 'nature' of managerial knowledge

This study sets popular management books in focus. But it is important to bear in mind that this is only one form of manifestation in which management knowledge is represented and diffused. In fact, all manifestations of management are textualisations of managerial life. Thus there are a vast number of oral or written packages dealing with what management is supposed to be. Some manifestations, such as books, attain great popularity, which means that they are also widely disseminated. Popular books therefore, it can be argued, represent a form of knowledge that many people are quite familiar with because it is the form of knowledge they are most likely to encounter, whether they do it intentionally or not.

Although popular books are only one way of packaging management knowledge, a particular book may circulate widely around the globe. This does not, however, render its content more truthful or representative of better and more useful knowledge than other less popular books. Thus, although some manifestations are very widely circulated, this in itself does not constitute what knowledge about management really is. It is also difficult to find ways of packaging knowledge in order for it to be moved in time and space without losing its relevance.

In the above example of the inhabitants' and the seafarers' different ways of representing the coastline (the myth and the map) it was argued that the meaning of these different representations of reality could be the same. Thus both inhabitants and seafarers might avoid the dangerous waters after hearing a story or reading a map. The important point here is the difference between the meaning and the representation of knowledge, i.e. it is possible that neither inhabitants nor seafarers would be likely to acquire relevant knowledge of this particular setting by access to the others' representation, since they are products of different discourses. Consequently, it can be argued that there are several representations in our modern society which are more or less accepted in different social networks. This means that when focusing on management knowledge we cannot define its universal, 'true meaning', but we can still discuss its 'nature'. This is also a delicate dilemma, and the complexity of the topic is articulated by Mintzberg (1991: 103):

> We live in societies obsessed with management. ... We idolize managers; we fill bookstores with studies of them, under 'fiction' as well as 'business'; we pretend to train huge numbers of innocent students to become them; we have even created a special class for

them in our airlines. Yet we cannot come to grips with the simple reality of what they do. Why?

By the same token he also writes 'today we sit with various lists of what managers do but virtually no serious theory' (*ibid.*: 99). In particular he means that there is a lack of empirically proved theories. His focus is mainly on how managers act, and he has argued elsewhere (Mintzberg 1973) that they tend to devote much of their effort to reacting to situations and occasions rather than to devising plans for the future or making decisions (cf. also Carlson 1951, 1991; Stewart 1967). However, despite these findings he points out that the task of modern management is still presented as 'POSDCORB' (Planning, Organising, Structuring, Directing, COordinating, Reporting, Budgeting), which was first formulated by Gulick and Urwick in 1937. This implies that the still dominating formula of what managers should do and what many of us believe that they actually do, is that success in business emanates from management's skills in decision making, planning, organising and controlling. But can we be so sure that this is what they really do? Even though there has been an expansion of studies in management, it is hard to say if there is actually a more uniform core of knowledge, or as Perrow (1986: 52) puts it, 'all the resources of organisational research and theory today have not managed to substitute better principles. ... We have more now, but they are no more scientific or useful than the classical ones'. The main reason may be that the 'nature' of knowledge in social science in general is that it uses everyday terms and deals with everyday life. Thus it elaborates on what people do every day, and since they do it they also know about it. Moreover, it is not as easy to define situations in management that are as dangerous as the case of medieval seafarers discussed above.

The complexity of knowledge production in the scientific field of management studies is stressed by Whitley (1984a: 90–1), who says that this subject is characterised by low mutual dependence and high task-uncertainty among scientists, i.e. there is neither one core of methods and knowledge which needs to be absorbed by scholars in the field, nor a consensus regarding what the tasks really are, and that:

> researchers are able to make contributions to a variety of goals without needing to incorporate specific results and ideas of particular specialist colleagues in a systematic way. They can deal with fairly broad problems and issues in a relatively diffuse manner and do not have to demonstrate exactly how their contribution fits

in with those of other members of that field. ... Groups in these sorts of fields form around diffuse and general problem areas which are often characterized as commonsense and everyday terms and are fairly fluid in membership and identities. ... Competence standards tend to be relatively informal and diffuse with different groups interpreting them differently so that co-ordination of results between research sites relies heavily on personal contact and knowledge.

Whitley points out that low mutual dependence and the use of everyday terms is typical of many of the social sciences, but perhaps most significant in Anglo-Saxon sociology and management research. These scientific fields constitute one extreme type which he defines as a 'fragmented adhocracy', since 'research is rather personal, idiosyncratic, and only weakly co-ordinated across research sites ... [and researchers] tend to make relatively diffuse contributions to broad and fluid goals which are highly contingent upon local exigencies and environmental pressures' (*ibid.*: 159). The opposite extreme in this argumentation is what Whitley calls twentieth-century physics after 1945, where specialist groups have developed differentiated goals which they pursue by means of standardised procedures. In this respect natural science stands out as a more organised and structured world than social science, since it is possible to prove that something is 'true' and something else is 'false'.

This view of knowledge seems to be a common model for what in general is meant by 'real' knowledge. However, the fact that the scientific field of physics is more structured and organised, on the basis of a single core of theory and methodology, does not mean that attempts to replicate it in social science will guarantee the development of more 'solid' or 'true' knowledge. This question is extensively discussed by McCloskey (1986: e.g. 24–7) who argues that the development of knowledge by means of predestined sophisticated methods is likely to have the result that what is sought is also what will be found. McCloskey means explicitly that this is the case in economics, but examples in this regard can also be found in other social science disciplines.

If we view this from the premise in the previous section, that knowledge in social science is judged according to its social relativity (Berger and Luckmann 1967), for an argument to be regarded as 'credible knowledge' in economics it needs to deal with a battery of well tried and accepted methods (McCloskey 1986: ch. 2). Otherwise, the argument will not be considered credible since it does not conform to the institutionalised enactment of standards for what 'knowledge' in the area is supposed to be. This will, however, not make such an argument more objectively true even though economists, according to McCloskey, tend to believe so. Economics is in this respect an extreme in the social sciences, since its arguments are mainly articulated with exact language codes tightly linked to mathematics. Thus, following Whitley (1984a: 90–1), it seems that the nature of management knowledge tends rather to the opposite extreme, since almost any argument can be given legitimacy as 'knowledge' as long as it is accepted as credible in any one particular social context.

To sum up, the nature of management knowledge can be defined as based on commonsense and described in everyday terms. In this regard, different social contexts are likely to have their own codes of acceptance and thereby particular discourses, i.e. established forms in which to converse (cf. McCloskey 1986: 27–8) on management and leadership issues. This means that within these discourses there are institutionalised codes for communication to which people turn when judging whether or not a manifestation is to be regarded as knowledge. In other words, there are likely to be established forms of rhetoric to represent managerial events in different social networks which give an argument the status of representing knowledge or not. It therefore seems reasonable to state that the form of argument given legitimacy is that which reflects and articulates the socially constructed norms of what management is supposed to be in that particular context. This means that within certain discourses certain kinds of representation are likely to be accepted as mobile, stable, and combinable. However, this need not signify that they are accepted as such in other discourses. For instance, arguments developed with an academic rhetoric are likely to be accepted as knowledge in academia, while in practice they may be judged as esoteric and not connected with reality. The converse may also be true, namely that academics see the arguments of practitioners, consultants and journalists as simplistic and not representing knowledge since they do not discuss methodologies and references.

An important question in this regard is: when is a manifestation qualified to represent knowledge? As will be argued below, this complexity can be discussed in terms of rhetoric, where one extreme represents knowledge and another ideology.

## Management knowledge and the production of managerial manifestations

Following the above argument, the development of managerial knowledge can be defined as a process of transforming observations and interpretations of social events into language codes which are given, or not given, legitimacy in particular discourses. Thus whether or not a phenomenon will be accepted as knowledge depends on how well it corresponds to institutionalised modes of representing knowledge. In particular this means that it is by language that knowledge, beliefs, myths, institutions and ideology are summarised and transferred from one situation to another. When interpretations are combined in order to be diffused as representations of certain observations, it can be argued that a text has been created, or that reality has been textualised (Bloomfield and Vurdobakis 1994). Latour (1987) adopts a similar approach when he discusses the creation of scientific texts in technoscience. He states that scholars use texts, files, documents, articles, etc. to persuade others that what was first an opinion has been transformed into a 'fact'. In this regard creators (authors) of texts use rhetoric to 'close' the argument and thus to be convincing. However, behind the creation of a text lies a process of observation, interpretation and selectivity.

Texts emanate from specific situations, and represent certain parts or elements of different social processes. These situations and processes are continuously observed and interpreted by both individuals and collectives. This means that different texts regarding these social processes are produced continuously. These texts are also continuously articulated, written down, read and interpreted by all participants in narrow and wider discourses. Therefore it can be argued that there is an ongoing discussion of management within organisations, organisational fields, societal sectors, nations and the global society. These collective discussions result in various texts that are continuously produced, read, ignored and interpreted.

Consequently, it can be argued that the specific features of written texts in this respect are that first, they articulate certain views of reality; and second, that they are packaged and distributed by the author in a perpetual format. In this respect written texts may function as tools whereby ideas, thoughts, ideology and knowledge are diffused at both macro level (the society or the organisational field) and micro level (small groups like organisations). Thus texts are, as Giddens (1979) writes, a particular form of language by which people communicate.[3]

So, management knowledge is developed in three steps: observation of a phenomenon, analyses of this phenomenon, and finally textualisation of the results in different forms of manifestation. First, something is observed in some way, then these observations are analysed in order to find patterns and dependent and independent variables. Finally, the observations and analyses are transformed into texts. Packaged into texts, this knowledge is then able to be diffused through space and time. In an ideal world the final text would represent the truth about the observed object. However, there are several complexities embodied in all these processes.

First, it is not possible to physically observe management processes! Actions taken by managers and those who are managed can be observed, and so also perhaps can their changes of behaviour over time, but the relationship between what managers and the managed do and the ultimate performance of the organisation, is not possible to observe physically. This means that there is always space for a great many interpretations of what is really happening in organisations.

Second, analyses can never be done objectively, with fresh eyes. Everything is observed through the filter of previous experience and knowledge gained elsewhere. This means that initially attention is drawn to predetermined aspects, whether or not this attention is outspoken or conscious. Then, what has been observed in this way is analysed in the same way; that is, interpretations are made through the filter of what is already known by the observer and others who have made observations and analyses of similar situations and objects.

Finally, what cannot be seen and what is analysed through the filter of the already-known is transformed into, and manifested by, texts. The relationship between thoughts and texts is complicated. It is very difficult to transform observations and analyses into plain text without omissions and changes to the real meaning of important aspects of what really happened. This is especially complicated when the object under scrutiny cannot be seen and cannot be analysed as it is. Thus there are reasons to be suspicious of textualisations of management that claim to objectively represent true knowledge about how management works, or the best knowledge, or the way to success. Yet such claims and promises are commonplace in popular management books.

To summarise the points made in this section, the production of managerial manifestations and the development of managerial knowledge do not necessarily have to correspond, since there are many complexities involved from the observation of a phenomenon to its textualisation. Below this dilemma is developed further when we take into account what happens when managerial manifestations are diffused.

## The diffusion of management knowledge and the distribution of managerial manifestations

The transmission in time and space of management knowledge is a complicated process. However, the distribution of managerial manifestations is easier to assimilate, since they are a form of package in which representations of management are transported. The transmission both of knowledge and manifestations is often discussed in terms of the diffusion of knowledge. This is, however, a concept that has its weaknesses when the relations between the development of management knowledge and the production, distribution and consumption of managerial manifestations are in focus. Technological innovations are natural objects which can be moved physically over time and space. A machine can, for instance, be used at one time or another, and be moved from where it was constructed and put into use somewhere else; and one can remain quite sure of its functions. A machine that is constructed in order to produce paper out of wood will probably do that rather than produce steel even if it is moved between locations and reproduced in many copies. Innovations in management, however, can hardly be seen as natural objects as can the papermaking machine. As discussed above, you can never be sure that managerial manifestations which claim to represent innovations will work in accordance with their claims when they are taken from the context in which they were produced and applied in another context. In fact, one cannot even be sure that they represent what really happened in that context, since there is a long journey from what really happened to the manifestation which claims to represent what happened. This means that the diffusion of representations of social events, such as how management and leadership work, is more complex than that of technological innovations since more ambiguous elements and relations between elements are involved. To talk in terms of the diffusion of management knowledge is thereby complicated. How can something that is not definite in its nature be diffused? Diffusion means that there is some kind of centre from where things are spread and that these things retain their form wherever they go. But if there is no centre then the diffusion concept becomes problematic. The distribution of a manifestation of how management works, however, can be described in terms of diffusion, at least as long as we focus only on the physical distribution of such a manifestation, and not on how the ideas it carries may be translated into actions.

Chapter 1 claimed that the considerable popularity of manifestations of management and leadership issues in modern western society was due to a few management gurus. These gurus represent one important group of a wider core of people and organisations which primarily seek to produce and diffuse manifestations of management. These are management consultants, teachers and researchers connected with business schools and universities, and business journalists. Due to the authority they are given in different social networks they can be seen as significant carriers of particular manifestations. Meyer (1996) calls these categories of actors, together with other categories of actors such as international governmental and non-governmental organisations, as 'others', since an important aspect of their activities is to tell organisations in which they are not involved what to do. Although there are great differences in what all categories of actors do in their daily work, there is one aspect that unites them, namely that an important dimension of their activities is to transmit representations of management. Thus they professionally produce manifestations and distribute them to practitioners, students, colleagues, readers and listeners. This means that managerial manifestations are transferred from one place to another consciously by groups of professional others. However, manifestations are also carried between places unconsciously, via spontaneous interaction in practice between individuals or in relation to formal business interchange. Consequently we all participate in a general worldwide process of transportation of managerial manifestations between organisations and societies, since we listen, observe, read, learn by experience and interpret everything around us. Then we talk, write and act in ways which bring our textualised interpretations and experience from one time and place to another.

So, the movement between locations of managerial manifestations is a complex subject, since these manifestations are transported via many routes, carried by many categories of actor and appear in many forms. However, it can be argued that the localisation of dominant voices in the popular discourse creates informal centres. To be more precise, observations have been made that Boston is the centre for all new ideas, since all management gurus have some connection with either Harvard University or the many large, international management consulting firms that have their headquarters there (Björkman 1997). This conclusion must, however, not be seen as definite.

The diffusion concept may be possible to use when the physical movement of popular manifestations is in focus, but it becomes more problematic when transmission of the content of these manifestations is taken into account, especially if we believe what Giddens (1979: 40–1) says: there is no single reading of a text since a reader always brings more to a text than its literal contents. To see texts in this way is in contrast to the traditional meaning of the diffusion of knowledge, which is that the readers passively accept the literal meaning of a manifestation. This is also what Whitley (1985) describes as the most common view of the popularisation of knowledge. In other words 'popularisation' means that the creator or other scholars actively diffuse the 'knowledge' and teach the 'facts' which are accepted in the literal meaning in which they were articulated by their creator. In this regard the receivers are supposed to 'learn' the 'facts'. Thus the receivers are not seen as participators in a negotiation about the meaning of a fact in a text, and the meaning of a text is seen as diffused when it has been taught to, or read by, a student (receiver) and no re-negotiation of the meaning of the facts is expected (cf. Latour 1987: e.g. 136–44). However, if a text does not have the same meaning in different contexts, the relevance of this view of the diffusion of management knowledge can be questioned.

## Management knowledge and black boxes

To talk in terms of the diffusion of innovations and knowledge in social science, and thereby also management studies, is complicated. Of course there is progress, and of course there are a great many people out there who do nothing else but diffuse various forms of packaged management knowledge. In this respect it seems fair to talk in terms of diffusion, i.e. the movement of manifestations of management in time and space via the actions taken by different categories of professionals. These actors can then be called professional carriers of knowledge. Management knowledge is thereby treated as something that can be packaged into black boxes and then be distributed across time and space while retaining its original meaning. However, as implied here and as will be discussed more in detail below, it can be argued that when we talk of how the meanings of management knowledge travel in time and space, concepts such as diffusion and black boxism are problematic.

Latour (1987: e.g. 132–44) criticises the traditional way of regarding the diffusion of innovations. Even though he makes his observations in the field of technoscience, the criticism he raises is also relevant in social science. Latour maintains that the traditional perspective sees 'knowledge' as something which can be packed into a 'black box' that can be applied by its recipients simply by adding the required input. In other words, this would mean that if the right input is added in the right way, for example to a management model suggested in a popular management book, the right output will automatically ensue. The requested output is usually organisational success. In this traditional approach, the knowledge is regarded as having a single unique meaning which can be defined and packed into a 'black box' and then diffused as 'closed' facts from one context to another. Thus the receivers of the black box in the 'new' context are said to be able to apply its contents literally as presented and described.

Latour's point is that the mere fact that the innovation has been physically conveyed to a receiver does not mean that all its capacities have been transmitted, or that the receiver will actually use it in accordance with its creator's intentions. In the diffusion model, black boxes are regarded as sets of indisputable facts which may not, and need not, be re-negotiated. This view of knowledge is well established in modern society and thus has many supporters. But this conception of knowledge has its limitations. It ignores the fact that it is individuals who construct, carry and receive knowledge, and that manifestations of management are continuously interpreted, re-interpreted and translated, whether or not we are aware of this.

Following the argument above, it becomes obvious that it is necessary to distinguish between the production and the consumption side of managerial manifestations. The former refers to processes where manifestations are produced and carried from place to place by certain actors, while the latter refers to the complex processes by which manifestations are de-contextualised and transmitted to individuals and organisational processes elsewhere. A manifestation might very well be diffused physically in a package such as a speech or a text. However, this physical movement of a manifestation does not mean that its meaning has been transmitted, although this is what the diffusion model suggests. Thus the physical journey across time and space of managerial manifestations is one thing, and the 'mental' journey another. Consequently, although it can be argued that there is a limited set of management models to choose from in the western world (DiMaggio and Powell 1983 [1991]), this does not necessarily mean that organisations around the globe have become homogeneous. In organisational studies, both the production and the consumption side of management knowledge are neglected areas. However, if we want to understand the paradox of homogeneous ideas and divergent behaviour in organisations, we need to go both backwards and forwards from the textualised ideas. This suggests that we need to deal with the processes of production and consumption of management knowledge. This study concentrates on the production side. Not because it is more important than the latter, but because little attention has been paid to it in organisation studies thus far. The remainder of this chapter will, however, focus on the consumption of management knowledge. In fact, in the 1990s the consumption side has been the subject of several studies where it has been argued that ideas are translated as they are consumed by an organisation.

## The consumption of managerial manifestations

It may seem inconvenient to use the term consumption when we talk about what the buyer of a managerial manifestation then does with their purchase. A managerial manifestation is not a product that can be drunk, eaten or used as a tool, and it does not actually disappear after it is consumed. The fact that someone has bought a managerial manifestation does not necessarily mean that they have applied or used it, or that they will do so in future. Instead, the practical use of different kinds of manifestations is probably the consequence of people's interpretations. Moreover, there are different types of manifestation. For instance, a book is in a more lasting format than advice from a consultant, a management seminar, or a management development programme. The book can be taken from the bookshelf whenever and be read over and over again, while the other manifestations are 'delivered' at one particular event. Nevertheless, although a book can be repeatedly read, it might very well happen that it is never taken from the shelf, and simply stored there; people may instead be more prone to apply what they have heard at a seminar or experienced in a management development programme. However, the fact that they have heard something is not necessarily the same as using or applying it in practice. Instead they may be more likely to 'consume' it as entertainment, which also might be the case with the reading of books.

In other words, by 'consume' we here refer to the manifestations which, due to their wide dissemination and great popularity, are what people in general are most likely to listen to, read and invest money in. What they do with them afterwards, i.e. whether they actually incorporate ideas provided in popular managerial manifestations into their behaviour, is more complicated to observe.

Thus the consumption of management books can take different forms, which also means that they may not always transmit their content to the consumer, at least not in the literal version. What we here label the consumption of managerial manifestations has been examined in several other studies. Røvik (1998a; 1998b) summarises the state of the art of studies where the introduction of ideas into organisations is considered. He argues that neither the idea of isomorphism as suggested by the new-institutionalists (e.g. DiMaggio and Powell 1983 [1991]) or of immunity as suggested by old-institutionalists (e.g. Selznick 1957) provides an accurate account of what actually happens when organisations attempt to introduce new management ideas. Røvik means that neither of these theories take into account the local processing or translation of ideas when they are transported between places and introduced into new situations. In the previous chapter, it was argued that the new institutional organisational analyses often suggest that the existence of widespread ideas triggers isomorphism among organisations in the global society through coercive, mimetic, cognitive and normative mechanisms. Certain ideas are thereby believed to be installed in organisations in the same way everywhere. As a result, organisations are believed to become isomorphic. The old-institutionalists, on the other hand, hold that organisations are integral units with distinct values and norms of their own. These values and norms are socialised in organisations and make them immune to ideas that do not fit, it is argued. Therefore, in contradiction to the new-institutionalists, the old-institutionalists suggest that organisations tend to reject popular ideas.

Nevertheless, although external ideas may clash with internal beliefs and complexities, there may still be a pressure from the environment to adopt them. This means that many organisations face the dilemma of efficiency on the one hand and being a legitimate actor in their field on the other. Sometimes these elements can go hand in hand, but not always. It might, for instance, happen that they need to demonstrate that they are modern and rational at the same time as needing to run the business as usual. In this way organisations have to meet claims from the environment that may very well be inconsistent. The decoupling of actions, decisions and talk may be the way to handle such inconsistencies (Meyer and Rowan 1977, 1991; Brunsson 1989); in this way organisations can act to satisfy some claims while making decisions or talk to satisfy others. What the organisation says may, for example, correspond to popular ideas, which means that popular management knowledge might very well be adopted in organisational talk in order to present the organisation as a legitimate actor in its field. Specific contextual circumstances, however, may force the organisation to make decisions and act in a way that clashes with this image.

Rejection and decoupling are two ways in which managerial manifestations can be consumed. However, as argued in several recent studies of the transmission of management ideas, it is also possible that they migrate into organisational activities. It is however, unlikely that they travel as black boxes; instead it has been observed that organisational recipes are translated wherever they go.

## The translation of managerial manifestations

The translation concept stems from dissatisfaction with the diffusion model as discussed above. Latour's (1987) criticism of the traditional view of the diffusion of knowledge in technoscience has in this regard been of great inspiration to students of organisations. He sees the spread in time and space of things and 'knowledge' of things as processes of translation. Thus he introduces the complexity whereby people in general interpret reality, and on the basis of their interpretations enact (cf. Weick 1979a; 1979b) how things work and their social meaning. Following Latour, it can therefore be argued that individuals tend to re-negotiate the meaning of the 'facts' diffused to them physically. Consequently, the fact that a manifestation of something has been diffused physically from one context to another, need not signify that its literal content has also been transmitted.

According to Latour, 'real' transmission, i.e. when meanings travel in time and space, occurs when participants in the new context translate the 'knowledge' into some kind of action that gives it significance for them. Transformation of knowledge is thereby a subjective process (cf. Berger and Luckmann 1967: 176), and the notion that ideas can be copied from one context to another can thereby be questioned. Thus, although a creator of a text 'closes' the arguments – i.e. packages the arguments in models which are structured as black boxes (rational input-process-output relations) – the receivers judge them in terms of their local usefulness.

This translation could thereby take different forms: from borrowing models and words when talking of management and leadership, to using models to structure and organise activities and events. The translation concept, as used here, is rather wide. However, Røvik (1998a; 1998b) has outlined a theory of the translation of organisational recipes where its meaning is more specific. He poses three questions: Where are the translations usually carried out? Why are popular ideas translated? How are they translated?

Translation may take place either within organisations or in their environment. Røvik (1998a; 1998b) suggests in this regard three different levels for translation: the field, in translation chains, and within organisations. When discussing the field level he says that there are authoritative centres in the the field that undertake translation and adaptation of popular recipes. Such centres work partly as a filter that sometimes excludes all other aspects of the recipe bar the field-specific version. Examples of such central actors are dominant consultancies in the field, or organisations that are specialised in certain expert roles. One example is national standardisation bodies who authorise quality recipes like ISO 9000. Such centres could be compared to what Meyer (1996) means by generalised others.

Nevertheless, translations are not only made by dominant actors in the field; we can also talk about translation in chains where a constant filtering and reinterpretation takes place at every link in the chain. A possible scenario might be that a recipe enters a field and there becomes translated by authoritative centres. When this field-specific recipe is adopted it becomes reinterpreted and translated by consultants or certain actors within local organisations into organisation-specific versions. When this version is introduced into the organisation, several translated versions are likely to be developed in all units of the organisation. Hence new local versions are likely to be created constantly wherever a recipe travels.

Next, in the process of implementing a recipe, further translations take place. Such processes are often run by managers or hired consulting firms who make their translations and then struggle to install them in the organisation. Special positions can also be established for experts whose task it is to adapt, for example, TQM and ISO 9000 to a organisation-specific quality management programme. Examples of such positions are quality managers, chief of quality or quality controller.

Following Røvik it can be argued that it is translations on the field level, namely the field actors and their translated versions, that are the focus of this study. As just mentioned, however, these actors are just links in a chain of translations.

Røvik does not only pay attention to where translation takes place; he also discusses the reasons why translation takes place. Possible explanations are that organisations tend to translate popular recipes either as a rationally calculated move, unintendedly, or as a way to manage identity. The first explanation suggests that certain elements from a recipe are extracted and adapted to local conditions based on calculations of what is needed to become efficient and gain economic rewards. It might also happen that managers recognise that to implement the recipe completely would require too much structural change, demand too many resources and pose too heavy a strain on the members of the organisation. Other calculated reasons might be that translations are made in order to avoid criticism or costly conflicts. Although not studied by Røvik, such calculations are likely to be made by all categories of actors in the translation chain, i.e. not only actors in local organisations. The second reason, however, gives a contradictory explanation by suggesting that translation might happen unintendedly. Even though the organisation may try very hard to copy a recipe and install it literally, it is still common for it to end up in a transformed version. One reason for this is that managers have limited time and capacity to consider all aspects of a recipe. Another reason is that popular recipes are de-contextualised, and when an organisation attempts to install one they cannot copy all of its aspects. It is, for instance, impossible to bring the weather or the infrastructure of California to Scandinavia, and vice-versa (cf. Sahlin-Andersson 1996). Moreover, it is also difficult to apply the characteristics of the hardware computer industry in Silicon Valley to the healthcare sector in Finland. Thus there are always many unintended translations going on by all categories of actors in the translation chain.

The third reason for translation mentioned by Røvik is the tendency to make a general management recipe like Total Quality Management (TQM) specific by developing local versions of it. In this way organisations signal their independence and uniqueness, since adopting popular ideas to the letter might be seen as a threat to the organisation's identity. Again, this local-specific translation can be made by different actors in the translation chain.

Thus far 'translation' has been used as a general term for the ways in which managerial manifestations may be given different meanings and appear in different versions when they travel in time and space. Røvik also discusses, however, how this can be understood, and says that translations appear in order of concretising, and as partly imitation, combination and remelting. By the first process he means that organisations often attempt to clarify a recipe and concretise it from being a general idea to a state of being embedded in the organisation's activities and routines. However, this is not the same as adopting the recipe as a whole. Perhaps it is more common that certain elements of the recipe are imitated while others are not considered or perhaps not transferable. It also happens that different recipes are combined, where elements are taken from each. The most radical form of translation can be called remelting, which means that various recipes are mixed and transformed into an entirely new variant. A similar analysis is made by Sahlin-Andersson (1996) when she argues that organisational recipes are edited wherever they travel, in each situation.

To conclude, when managerial manifestations such as distinct organisational recipes are consumed, i.e. when they travel to and become embedded in organisational activities and routines, then they are likely to be translated in different ways or even edited into completely different versions. This is also likely to take place in the chain of translation by all actors involved.

## Conclusions

In this chapter we have focused on management knowledge and the production, diffusion and consumption of managerial manifestations. In this regard one major argument is that managerial knowledge does not really possess a stable core of methods and standard works which scholars must penetrate before they can claim to give contributions. Several different arguments can acquire legitimacy as long as they are accepted in a context. It seems to be the credibility attached to them by their audience which determines whether they are to be regarded as knowledge or not. If we use this definition of the nature of management knowledge, then this has consequences for how we understand the development and movement of management knowledge in time and space. A second major argument is therefore that knowledge in the field, and manifestations thereof, can be understood as processes of interpretations and textualisations of observations of reality, where rhetoric is the 'method' of communication. In this regard the rhetoric used by the 'producer' of a managerial manifestation is important for whether it is to be accepted as knowledge or not. The nature of knowledge in the field also has consequences for how knowledge can be transmitted in time and space. A third major argument is therefore that the physical diffusion of knowledge is not the same thing as a receiver adopting its literal content. Diffusion can be a proper word for the transportation of manifestations, i.e. the physical distribution of packages of knowledge, while what people really comprehend depends on how they consume the manifestations they meet. This consumption can take different forms and then be undertaken for different reasons; it can take place at different levels and be carried out in different ways.

# 4 Trends in the supply of management books

## Introduction[1]

The purpose of this study is to analyse how popular management books are made and what they mean for organisations. In order to do this, a selection of books of particular significance will be analysed in detail. For this reason we shall in this chapter study the characteristics of the supply of books in Sweden in the 1980s. In this way important trends and patterns in the Swedish managerial discourse can be identified. Thereafter a few significant spokespersons for these trends, and a number of books written by these persons, can be selected for detailed studies, in later chapters, of the contents and production processes of popular books and what they mean for organisations. However, to discern the most significant spokesperson, i.e. to prove statistically that one person is more significant than another, is not easy. For instance, it is always difficult to gain access to detailed sales statistics from publishing houses. There are also problems in deciding whether or not a book is to be seen as a management book, and over what period the sales should be counted. For instance, if Barley and Kunda (1992) and Husczynski (1993) are right that old ideologies and ideas do not disappear from the general discourse, a book achieving great sales today may not be as prominent in the general managerial discourse as for example Taylor's book from 1911, Barnard's from 1938 or McGregor's from 1960. Besides, some of the bestsellers in the management book genre, such as autobiographies of famous business-men and managers like McCormack (1984), Iacocca (1984) and Geneen (1985), should probably be seen more as entertainment rather than as having any influence worthy of note on the general managerial discourse.

Consequently it may not be possible to prove statistically who the most significant spokespersons are, but when applying a social constructive approach to reality (cf. Berger and Luckmann 1967) as in the present study, this is not really a problem. The reason is that the significance of different managerial manifestations is regarded in this perspective as a consequence of their social relativity, i.e. the statistically most significant spokesperson may not be the same as the most significant reference in the general managerial discourse. So, the most appropriate way to discern significant spokespersons of the modern general managerial discourse will not necessarily be to use sophisticated statistical methods. However, statistics are useful, but it may be more appropriate to compare data from the supply of books through different channels than to focus only on their sales volumes. Therefore, statistics collected from different sources are used in this study, and comparisons are made between data from the supply of books in both the popular discourse and the academic. To discern a few spokespersons of particular significance, interpretations will be made instead of the application of advanced mathematics. We may thus be able to identify a few significant books which can be used later for more detailed analyses of the production of popular managerial manifestations.

Huczynski (1993) uses statistical sources to identify management gurus. Quantitative data are also used by Alvarez (1991) in his study of the diffusion and institutionalisation of organisational knowledge in Britain, Mexico and Spain. He collected statistics on economic and political crises, and on the diffusion of one concept in formal (business schools) and informal (media and books) education, governmental promotion and, in particular, business groups. Engwall (1992) also employed quantitative data in his analysis of the origin of literature used over time in teaching at the Stockholm School of Economics. Data of a similar kind are also collected in the present study, first to map general characteristics in the field of diffusion of managerial texts, and then to identify significant spokespersons. We can thereby search for characteristics of the origin of management books in general, but also among the most popular manifestations.

## General trends in the western managerial discourse

Are there other trends apart from the infamous Americanisation? Engwall (1992) points out that up to World War II, Swedish management education at least was influenced by the German tradition, but that thereafter there has been a shift away from Germanism to Americanism.

The UK and France were probably less Germanised in this regard than Sweden, but similar trends to the Swedish one can be observed in several other countries, such as the other Scandinavian states and the Netherlands. In the Netherlands, however, the German tradition was never really abandoned even though the American influence has gradually increased (cf. de Man 1995).

In this chapter the diffusion of management books in the western world is analysed from a Swedish viewpoint. There are, however, good reasons to believe that Sweden is no exception. This means that the Swedish case can be seen as an illustration of more general patterns. The study is primarily limited to the 1980s, which can be seen as an illustrative period in the popularity of management knowledge, due to the expansion of the industry in several dimensions (e.g. books, consultancies and seminars) during this period.

To identify significant spokespersons is not unproblematic, since the significance of a book can be seen as a consequence of its social relativity in different situations. This means that the most sold book is not necessarily the most significant for the agenda of the general managerial discourse. Sales statistics give information on sales volumes and thereby on the physical diffusion of books. However, they provide no information on whether the highest-selling books were 'translated' by individuals and are thereby important when people converse about management. To handle this complexity, this study does not only rely on sales statistics to discern the significance of particular books. Instead, the data presented in this chapter are collected from different sources, where the supply of books is mapped and we search for characteristics therein. No claim is made here to identify the most important spokespersons. The ambition is rather to discern a few books and authors which appear to be representative of significant patterns in the supply of popular books.

First we shall try to identify characteristics of the general supply. Data on management books acquired by, and stored in registers and databases at Swedish libraries are used for this purpose. We compare patterns in the stock of books before 1980 with patterns thereafter, and also scrutinise the annual increase of books in the 1980s in search of characteristics of the diffusion over the years. Second, the scope is narrowed to a search for characteristics of the diffusion of books in the popular discourse. We thereby arrive at a stock consisting solely of books which have attained a considerable diffusion. In particular we look for characteristics of the distribution of books by management book clubs, among those appearing on a bestseller list, and among the bestselling books according to sales statistics from publishing houses. We also analyse books that appeared in management teaching at Swedish universities and university colleges, where we try to particularise those most frequently used. By comparing characteristics from these different sources, we can identify a few spokespersons who are believed on good grounds to be significant representatives of the Swedish popular managerial discourse.

## General characteristics of the supply of management books

In order to observe general characteristics of the supply of management books in Sweden over time, the database IMDOC, containing most of the books stored in Swedish libraries, has been used. Some libraries use other classifications and are connected to other databases, which means that IMDOC does not contain all the books available. However, there are good reasons to believe that the 5,804 titles covered by IMDOC and thereby included in this study (Table 4.1) gives a representative view of the stock of books on management in Swedish libraries in the 1980s. This is probably the most comprehensive source for statistics on management books available in Sweden. It is thereby possible to obtain figures for the total stock of books classified under management (Qba) in the libraries connected to IMDOC, the origin of these books, and the annual increase of the stock. The general characteristics of this material are presented in Table 4.1.

*Table 4.1* The origin of book stocks on management in Swedish libraries

| Country | Total Number | % | -1980 Number | % | 1980–89 Number | % |
|---|---|---|---|---|---|---|
| Sweden | 2,251 | 39 | 865 | 35 | 1,386 | 42 |
| USA | 1,631 | 28 | 832 | 34 | 799 | 24 |
| Great Britain (GB) | 944 | 16 | 373 | 15 | 571 | 17 |
| Germany (FRG) | 244 | 4 | 127 | 5 | 117 | 3 |
| France | 50 | 1 | 20 | 1 | 30 | 1 |
| Sum | 5,120 | 88 | 2,217 | 90 | 2,903 | 87 |
| others | 684 | 12 | 256 | 10 | 428 | 13 |
| | | 100 | | 100 | | 100 |
| *Total no. published:* | 5,804 | 100 | 2,473 | 43 | 3,331 | 57 |

*Source*: Based on the Swedish libraries database IMDOC (13 February 1991).
*Note*: Figures state number of titles sorted under management (Qba-)

Table 4.1 shows that about half of the books (57 per cent) were published between 1980 and 1989. Furthermore, with respect to the supply's general characteristics, it also shows that about 39 per cent of the total number of books were published in Sweden, 28 per cent in the United

States, 16 per cent in the United Kingdom, 4 per cent in Germany, about 1 per cent in France and 12 per cent in other countries. However, worthy of note here is that the classification of a book according to nationality is based on its place of publication. This means that a book written by an American but translated into Swedish and published in Stockholm is thus considered as Swedish. Likewise a book classified as originating in the United States may have been written by a Swede. However, there is reason to believe that the translations of books into Swedish far outnumber those written by Swedes and published abroad. This indicates that the foreign influence is underestimated in the database used. However, with this in mind we can see from Table 4.1 that books published in Sweden, the US and Britain predominate, and that books published in non-anglophone countries (except Sweden) are negligible.

To acquire more detailed information on the yearly development during the 1980s, an investigation was also made of the numbers of books published annually between 1980 and 1989 in the three countries which dominate the field. These results are presented in Table 4.2, where it can be seen that during the 1980s the number of management titles registered each year in Swedish libraries steadily increased from 274 in 1981 to 425 in 1988.

*Table 4.2*    Publication of management books during the 1980s: a yearly development sketch

| Year | Published in: Total | Sweden Yearly no. | % | USA Yearly no. | % | GB Yearly no. | % |
|------|------|------|------|------|------|------|------|
| 1980 | 274 | 75 | 27 | 84 | 31 | 30 | 11 |
| 1981 | 202 | 79 | 39 | 50 | 25 | 36 | 18 |
| 1982 | 250 | 101 | 40 | 64 | 26 | 40 | 20 |
| 1983 | 299 | 132 | 44 | 73 | 24 | 51 | 17 |
| 1984 | 313 | 137 | 44 | 82 | 26 | 46 | 15 |
| 1985 | 376 | 166 | 44 | 86 | 23 | 62 | 16 |
| 1986 | 378 | 174 | 46 | 83 | 22 | 61 | 16 |
| 1987 | 379 | 157 | 41 | 71 | 19 | 81 | 21 |
| 1988 | 435 | 189 | 43 | 100 | 23 | 85 | 20 |
| 1989 | 425 | 176 | 41 | 106 | 24 | 79 | 19 |
| *Sum:* | 3,331 | 1,386 | 42 | 799 | 24 | 571 | 17 |

*Source*: IMDOC, 13 February 1991

The proportion of books published each year in the US fluctuated between 19 and 31 per cent. The average for the 1980s amounts to 24 per cent, which corresponds fairly well to the magnitude of the share of

American books in the total library stock (28 per cent). It is interesting that it also corresponds to the figures mentioned by Engwall (1992: 156) in his study of business administration as an academic and a practical discipline, regarding the share of American textbooks used in teaching at the Stockholm School of Economics (25 per cent in 1985). However, it is also worthy of note that the relative share of books from the US peaked in 1980 (31 per cent) and that since 1981 it has been relatively stable at around 25 per cent, apart from a drop in 1987 to 19 per cent. The annual share of books published in Sweden fluctuated between 27 and 46 per cent, while the average was 42 per cent. This is contrary to the development among books from the US, since the lowest annual share in Sweden appeared in 1980 (27 per cent). Nevertheless, as in the US, the level since 1981 has been stable, between 39 and 46 per cent. However, the annual share of books originating in Britain is more variable. The average was 17 per cent for the whole period, while the annual share fluctuated between 11 and 20 per cent. As in the case of the Swedish books, the lowest share appeared in 1980 (11 per cent), and the figure was 18 per cent in 1981. Between 1983 and 1986 the British share scored around 16 per cent, and in 1987 it stabilised at around 20 per cent.

To conclude, the data presented in both tables confirm that the supply of management books in general is dominated by books published in Sweden, the US and to some extent the UK, and that books with other origins are nearly non-existent. The observations also support the notion of an increase in the interest in management issues during the 1980s. Moreover, the share of Swedish and American books was stable from 1981 onward, while the share of British books varied. These results imply that the general managerial discourse can be characterised, since there is also, alongside of local, nationally published books, a considerable impact from books with a British or, especially, an American origin.

## Characteristics of the supply of popular books

So far the material described includes all the books in Swedish libraries classified under 'management': namely academic papers, textbooks, and books designed for practitioners. As can be seen in Tables 4.1 and 4.2, the stock of books published in the 1980s amounted to 3,331. To study the production of all these in detail is unfortunately not possible, and therefore a smaller population must be identified which is more relevant in regard to dominant perspectives. Therefore, with the results above in mind we shall now concentrate on the popular managerial discourse, where observations will be made on books distributed by management book clubs, books that appeared on a bestseller list in a management magazine, and the highest-selling books according to publishers' sales statistics.

## Books distributed through management book clubs

Literature distributed by book clubs specialising in management is primarily circulated to managers and others interested in managerial issues. Moreover, companies and organisations often receive the books on subscription and circulate them among their staff. This is an indication that the books are widely exposed to practitioners and probably also in one way or another 'consumed' by many. Here we shall look for the characteristics of the origin of books via three of the most important Swedish management book clubs, and compare these with the characteristics of the general supply presented above.

As early as 1977, Liber, the first Swedish publishing firm, founded the Liber Management Club – Bättre Ledarskap (Improved Leadership). The credo of the club appears on the dustjacket of books which they distribute in this way. Here, among others, they cite Normann (1983): 'The real winners choose improved leadership'. They also claim to seek 'those of you who see ideas and knowledge as the most effective tools for achieving your goals'. The imprint's intention is to review international publications in the field and choose the best, even though they want as many Swedish books as possible on their list. However, at least two other management book clubs were in operation in the 1980s, the Svenska Dagbladets Executive Book Club, established in 1983, and Chefens Bokklubb (The Manager's Book Club, Timbro) established in 1985. They both had objectives similar to those of Liber's book club.

These book clubs altogether distributed about 140 different titles in the 1980s. As shown in Table 4.3, of these almost 50 per cent were written by Americans, 45 per cent by Swedes and only 5 per cent by other nationals. Every second book originated in the US, and this could be interpreted as an indication of the great influence which that country exercises on management thinking among Swedish practitioners. There are, however, some differences between the book clubs. Timbro, for instance, offers predominantly Swedish books, while the other two have opposite priorities. However, these differences are not substantial.

*Table 4.3*   The origin of the authors of books supplied by management
book clubs

| Country | Total number | % of total |
|---------|:---:|:---:|
| USA | 70 | 50 |
| Sweden | 63 | 45 |
| Others | 7 | 5 |
| *Sum:* | 140 | 100 |

*Source*: IMDOC, 13 February 1991

If we compare the figures presented in Table 4.3 with the general view discussed in the previous paragraph, we can again see that books with a Swedish or American origin predominate. However, in this population the Americans are predominant while no book of British origin can be observed. This suggests that the more practical and popular the distribution channel, the higher the share of books of American origin.

## Books appearing on a Swedish bestseller list

In addition to the book clubs, the bestseller list in *Ledarskap* (*Leadership*), the leading Swedish management magazine of the 1980s, provides further information on popular management books. This list was first published in the October 1987 issue, and subsequently included in every issue until the magazine ceased publication in 1991. It was based on information from six of the leading specialist bookstores in Sweden.[2] Altogether, 156 titles written by 131 different authors have appeared on the list. Since many of the books on this list were also distributed through book clubs, there is reason to regard it as representing some of the most significant 'voices' in the popular managerial discourse of the 1980s.

Table 4.4 lists the titles of the twenty-two books which have appeared five times or more on *Ledarskap*'s bestseller list. The more often a book is mentioned on the list, the larger its circulation is presumed to be. In the period covered by the list, eight (36 per cent) of the twenty-two books were written by Americans, thirteen (59 per cent) by Swedes, and one by a Norwegian. Moreover, it is remarkable that none of the most popular books on the bestseller list, nor any of those distributed by the book clubs, altogether nearly 200 titles, are of British origin. This contrasts with the share of British management books in Swedish libraries as indicated in Table 4.1.

*Table 4.4*    Management books appearing more than five times on a Swedish bestseller list between 1987 and 1990

| | Origin of the author | | |
|---|---|---|---|
| *Title and Author* | *Am* | *Swe* | *Other* |
| 1. *Thriving on Chaos*, Peters, T., 1987 | X | | |
| 2. *In Search of Excellence*, Peters, T. & Waterman, R., 1982 | X | | |
| 3. *Kunskapsföretaget*, Risling J, & Svejby, K-E., 1986 | | X | |
| 4. *Utan Omsvep*, Ericsson C., 1987 | | X | |
| 5. *Odyssey: From Pepsi to Apple*, Sculley J., 1988 | X | | |
| 6. *High Visibility*, Kotler, P., Rein, I. & Stoller, M., 1988 | X | | |
| 7. *Unlimited Power*, Robbins, A., 1987 | X | | |
| 8. *Först till Framtiden*, Railo W., 1988 | | | X |
| 9. *Målförverkligande Ledarskap*, Wiberg, L. & Stemme, I., 1987 | | X | |
| 10. *Moments of Truth*, (Riv Pyramiderna), Carlzon, J., 1985/1987 | | X | |
| 11. *Skapande Personalarbete*, Hansson J., 1988 | | X | |
| 12. *Business Strategy in Practice* (Strategins kärnfrågor), Karlöf, B., 1985 | | X | |
| 13. *Business Strategy* (Affärsstrategi), Karlöf B., 1989/1988 | | X | |
| 14. *Ledarutmaningen*, Karlöf, B, Söderberg, M., 1989 | | X | |
| 15. *Känn dig som Ledare*, Norberg, L., 1987 | | X | |
| 16. *Ledning av Kunskapsföretaget*, Alvesson, M., 1989 | | X | |
| 17. *Quality is Free*, Crosby, P. 1988 | X | | |
| 18. *Trender i 90-talets Näringsliv*, Wahlström, B., 1988 | | X | |
| 19. *Initiativets Makt*, Lindstedt, M., 1985 | | X | |
| 20. *Leadership Secrets of Attila the Hun*, Roberts, W., 1989 | X | | |
| 21. *Kunskapsföretagets Marknadsföring*, Arnell, B-M. & Nico, M., 1989 | | X | |
| 22. *Boone*, Boone Pickens, T., 1987 | X | | |
| *22 titles (20 authors)* | 8 | 13 | 1 |
| *% of total* | 36 | 59 | 5 |

*Source*: Based on *Ledarskap*'s bestseller list, October 1987–October 1990
*Note*: Titles are listed in order of frequency of appearances on the list

Table 4.4 shows that two books written or co-authored by the American management consultant Tom Peters top the list. These are followed by two books written by Swedes where the first, *Kun-*

*skapsföretaget*, discusses knowledge-intensive firms and the second, *Utan Omsvep* (*Straight Out*) is a biographical 'defence' by a famous Swedish entrepreneur whose offshore company had remarkable success for several years but was eventually forced into bankruptcy. Then come three American books where the first, *Odyssey: from Pepsi to Apple* (Sculley 1988) is a biography of the author's successful careers in first Pepsi and later Apple. The second, *High Visibility*, is a book on the importance of marketing, while the third, *Unlimited Power*, draws on psychology and mysticism and discusses the power of self-confidence. Then a Norwegian book, *Först til Framtiden* (*First to the Future*) is listed. It is written by a professor of psychology and discusses the importance of self-confidence, goals and visions. It is followed by two Swedish books, where the first, *Målförverkligande Ledarskap* (*Leadership for Achieving Objectives*) also focuses on goals, while in the second we again find an autobiography in Jan Carlzon's *Moments of Truth* (see below).

The books just discussed are the ten most frequently appearing on *Ledarskap*'s bestseller list. It is interesting that five of these (50 per cent) were written by North Americans and four (40 per cent) by Swedes. However, the twelve books listed as numbers eleven to twenty-two show another pattern, where nine (75 per cent) are of Swedish origin and three (25 per cent) North American.

An analysis of the entire list yields another characteristic, that the list consists of a mix of books of different kinds. There are four autobiographies of famous managers, two of whom are Swedes (Carlzon 1985, 1987; Ericsson 1987) and two from the US (Pickens 1987; Sculley 1988). Moreover, five books are focused on goals, strategy and quality (Wiberg and Stemme 1987; Karlöf 1987, 1988; Crosby 1988; Railo 1988) and four on leadership (Norberg 1987; Wiberg and Stemme 1987; Karlöf and Söderberg 1989; Roberts 1989). There are also two books on knowledge-intensive firms (Risling and Svejby 1986; Alvesson 1989), two which are psychological in orientation (Robbins 1987; Railo 1988) and two which discuss management and organisation in general (Peters and Waterman 1982; Peters 1987). It is also worthy of note that three books were written or co-authored by the Swedish consultant Bengt Karlöf and two by the American consultant Tom Peters. Moreover, there is only one real 'outsider' on the list, namely *Ledning av Kunskapsföretaget* (Alvesson 1989) which is written in an academic tradition and with an academic rhetoric.

Thus, when well distributed books primarily directed at practitioners are approached, we only see one trend besides the local or national; namely Americanisation. Here we see no sign of books from the UK or elsewhere, in contrast to the general stock of Swedish libraries analysed above.

## The bestselling books in Sweden during the 1980s

To complete the above view of significant 'voices' in the popular discourse, sales statistics from publishing houses were collected. However, it proved difficult to obtain any reliable sales statistics from publishers or other institutions. Nevertheless, the books believed to be the highest-selling in Sweden during the 1980s are listed in Table 4.5. Sales volumes are based on information from publishers and cover the period up to 1989. The list includes books distributed by book clubs as well as those circulated through bookstores. According to these figures, by far the most successful book is *Riv Pyramiderna* (*Moments of Truth*) (Carlzon 1985 [1987]) written by Jan Carlzon, former managing director of the Scandinavian Airlines System, SAS. It was first published in 1985 and has so far sold 140,000 copies. It outnumbers the second book on the list by about 100,000. SAS and Jan Carlzon attracted considerable attention in Sweden and abroad as a result of the company's restructuring in the early 1980s.

The books in positions two to four all originate in the United States and were distributed through Svenska Dagbladets Executive Book Club. The second book on the list, *In Search of Excellence* (Peters and

*Table 4.5*    The highest-selling management books in Sweden

| Authors | Titles | A | S | V |
|---|---|---|---|---|
| Carlzon J. | *Moments of Truth* | | x | 140 |
| Peters & Waterman | *In Search of Excellence* | x | | 40 |
| Iacocca L. | *Iacocca: An Autobiography* | x | | 30 |
| Blanchard & Johnson | *The One Minute-Manager* | x | | 25 |
| Normann R. | *Service Management* | | x | 20 |
| Svejby & Risling | *Kunskapsföretaget* | | x | 20 |
| Karlöf B. | *Strategins kärnfrågor* | | x | 15 |
| Ericsson C. | *Utan Omsvep* | | x | 14 |
| *Per cent of the most sold books* | 38% | | 62% | |

*Source*: Figures are based on publishers' information and cover sales up to and including 1989.

*Note*: A = American; S = Swedish; V = volumes sold, thousands

Waterman 1982) achieved sales of about 40,000 in Sweden.[3] However, as mentioned earlier, it has according to Thomas (1989) sold more than ten million copies worldwide. It is followed by *Iacocca: An Autobiography* (Iacocca 1984) and *The One Minute-Manager* (Blanchard and Johnson 1982), with sales of 25–30,000 copies. Of the books mentioned here, two, Carlzon's and Iacocca's, can be classified as autobiographies, although Carlzon's book has a more theoretical approach; the rest can be called handbooks, since they contain normative advice on how to solve organisational problems.

The bestsellers among Swedish books belonging to the latter category are *Service Management* (Normann 1983), *Kunskapsföretaget* (*The Knowledge-Intensive Firm*) (Svejby and Risling 1986) and *Strategins Kärnfrågor* (*Business Strategy in Practice*) (Karlöf 1985) with sales of 15–20,000. However, according to Richard Normann himself, his doctoral dissertation from 1975, *Skapande Företagsledning* (*Management for Growth*) (1977) has sold even more copies than *Service Management*.[4] Interestingly enough, all the Swedish books mentioned have also been published abroad. The sales achieved by these books are extraordinary, at least in the light of what one publisher has said: 'we consider books with sales of more than 2,000 as successful books'.

To conclude: as in the other distribution channels discussed above, it is clear that the diffusion of management books in Sweden consists of sales of Swedish and American books. Carlzon's book is no doubt the highest selling. However, the second book is one of US origin, *In Search of Excellence*. The first, third and eighth titles on the list are autobiographies, while the others can be classified as handbooks. The second most popular Swedish book, and also the most widely circulated along with *Kunskapsföretaget*, was *Service Management*.

## Books used in academic management education

In order to obtain a broader outlook on which spokespersons to select for detailed studies of the contents and the production of popular managerial manifestations, an investigation was also made of a distribution channel in the academic discourse, namely literature used in teaching at Swedish universities and university colleges. The reason is that this distribution channel is important not only for authors, but also for its impact on the agenda of the general managerial discourse, since graduates bring their experiences from universities, university colleges and business schools with them when they enter employment. This source may not include the bestselling volumes, but consists of books which are actually read by many, and are also used practically by students to carry out tasks and solve problems as part of their studies.

Data were collected in order to study the origin of the most frequently used books. A list was then made of the set of books in courses on organisation, management and leadership in the business administration programme, and in special courses within business administration.[5] The study comprised all universities and university colleges in Sweden. In cases when it was difficult to decide whether a course could be placed within the above categories, the decision was based on whether or not concepts such as organisation, management, leadership, administration and strategy occurred in the course name. In addition, the tables of contents, the course-content descriptions and the titles of the available literature were examined.

The study showed that during the academic year 1991–2 there were 103 courses complying with the above criteria at Sweden's six universities, two business schools and nineteen university colleges. Among these about 50 per cent of the course titles included the concept 'organisation', about 20 per cent 'managing/leadership', about 15 per cent 'administration' and about 15 per cent 'management' or 'strategy'. On these 103 courses, 200 different books written by 177 different authors or constellations of authors were used, 56 per cent of whom were Swedes, 33 per cent Americans, 5 per cent Britons, 3 per cent Canadians and 3 per cent other nationals (Table 4.6).

*Table 4.6*    Origin of the authors of literature used in teaching at universities and university colleges

| Country | Total number | Per cent of total |
|---|---|---|
| Sweden | 112 | 56 |
| USA | 67 | 33 |
| Great Britain | 9 | 5 |
| Canada | 6 | 3 |
| Other | 6 | 3 |
| Total | 200 | 100 |

*Source*: A revision of results collected by Kragelund (1992).

To identify the most popular reading at institutes of higher education in Sweden, the books were counted with regard to the number of courses on which they were used. The data are summarised in Table 4.7 below. We can see that Normann (1975) tops the list, followed by Bruzelius and Skärvad (1988).[6] Then Mintzberg (1983), a Canadian, appears together with another book by Normann (1983). On dividing the literature into basic and advanced courses it was found that on basic courses, i.e. courses which all students of business administration must attend, summary books were preferred.

*Table 4.7* The most widely distributed books among universities and university colleges during the academic year 1991–2

| Author | Title | Appear on number of courses (frequency) | | | |
|---|---|---|---|---|---|
| | | Total | Basic course | Advanced course | Origin |
| Normann, R., 1975 | Skapande företagsledning | 15 | 3 | 12 | s |
| Bruzelius, & Skärvad, 1974/1988 | Integrerad organisationslära | 14 | 14 | | s |
| Mintzberg, H., 1983 | Structure in Fives | 11 | 8 | 3 | c |
| Normann, R., 1983 | Service Management | 11 | 6 | 5 | s |
| Bakka & Fivelsdal, 1988 | Organisationsteori – struktur, kultur, och processer | 7 | 4 | 3 | n, d |
| Morgan, G., 1986 | Images of Organization | 7 | 5 | 2 | c |
| Lennér et al., 1979 | Arbetsgruppens psykologi | 6 | 4 | 2 | s |
| Bengtsson & Skärvad, 1991 | Företagsstrategiska perspektiv | 5 | 4 | 1 | s |
| Granberg, O, 1989 | Personaladministra- tion och organisations utveckling | 5 | 4 | 1 | s |
| Sjöstrand, S-E, 1987 | Organisationsteori | 5 | 5 | | s |
| Alvesson, M., 1988 | Ledning av kunskapsföretaget | 4 | 4 | | s |
| Porter, M., 1985 | Competetive Advantage | 4 | | 4 | a |
| Schein, E., 1985 | Organizational Culture and Leadership | 4 | | 4 | a |

*Source*: The table is a revision of material collected by Kragelund (1992).

*Note*: d = Danish; c = Canadian; n = Norwegian; s = Swedish; a = American

As shown in the table, the most frequently used book was *Integrerad Organisationslära* (*Integrated Organisation Theory*) by Bruzelius and Skärvad (1988), which was used on fourteen courses. The second book on the list is *Structure in Fives* by Mintzberg (1983), used on eight courses. In third place we find Normann's *Service Management* (1983) appearing on six courses, and in fourth place, used on four courses, Bakka and Fivelsdal's *Organisationsteori: struktur, kultur, processer* (*Organisation Theory: Structure, Culture, Processes*) (1988).

An introductory course has of necessity a summary character. However, it is worthy of note that most students do not undertake further reading within this field, so that the opinions regarding organisations and organising, which they here encounter, can be expected to influence their future views.

On advanced courses, Normann's book *Skapande Företagsledning* (*Management for Growth*) predominates in the literature. The second book is *Service Management*, by the same author. Then follow two American books by Schein (1985) and Porter (1985), two Harvard professors who combine consultancy with research.

To conclude, a good half of the study literature used is written by Swedish authors and only one third by Americans. Out of the six most widely distributed books, two are of Canadian and four of Scandinavian origin, three of which are written by Swedish authors, Richard Normann alone being responsible for two of them.

## Conclusion: Americanisation and nationalism

It is evident from this study that the American influence on management books circulated in Sweden is very substantial. Moreover, with very few exceptions only American and Swedish-books are represented among them. It is, however, somewhat astonishing to find that there are no management books from Japan or Germany, despite their economic success during the period in focus here. It is also remarkable that books of British origin are more or less non-existent, bearing in mind their large share of books in the general supply of libraries, and that English is an easily accessible language for Swedes and many other nationalities. The American dominance may be due to the extensive investment in marketing by American publishing firms in combination with the success of American consultancy companies worldwide. Similar global strategies cannot be discerned in other countries like Japan and Germany. Another reason may be language-related, i.e. books from Japan and Germany, for example, are not translated into either English or Swedish. It could also be that books from these countries are rare or do not exist. It is true that a few Swedish management books have been translated into English, but this cannot be compared with the air of globalisation which pervades the American books. So, the origin of management books disseminated in Sweden seems, frankly, to be the US. However, this could also be interpreted to indicate that the only trend of global significance is that of Americanisation, and that each nation has its local gurus and a large share of domestically produced books. But the difference is that these domestically produced books are based on domestic references and local observations. In the next chapter we will elaborate more on this issue.

If a few significant spokespersons of the popular managerial discourse in Sweden during the 1980s are to be selected, it seems appropriate to search for authors who represent what is perhaps the most striking finding of the survey, namely the predominance of books of Swedish and American origin. In this regard there is no doubt that *In Search of Excellence* (Peters and Waterman 1982) is the most significant American book in the Swedish discourse, since it was singled out as the second highest-selling management book in Sweden in the 1980s. On top of that list Jan Carlzon's book was outstanding. However, it did not appear on the list of books used in higher manage-ment education. It was very obvious that there, Richard Normann's *Skapande Företagsledning* (*Management for Growth*, 1975 and 1977) and *Service Management* (1983) were of particular importance. If this is compared with the fact that *Service Management* was the second highest-selling Swedish book after Carlzon's, since Normann himself remarked that his 1975 book has sold in even higher quantities, and since the second most frequently used book in teaching in its original version was written when its authors (Bruzelius and Skärvad 1988) were his colleagues at the Swedish consulting firm SIAR, it seems that Richard Normann has been a significant source for several popular books of Swedish origin. The reasons are that his books are popular both in academic teaching and in general, and that other popular books appear to have been written in the same context. Moreover, the English title of Carlzon's book, *Moments of Truth*, is one of the core concepts in Normann's 1983 book!

Consequently, it seems appropriate to regard *In Search of Excellence* as representing the American tendency, and *Service*

*Management* the domestic. The authors of these books, Tom Peters and Robert Waterman, and Richard Normann, can thereby be seen as significant spokespersons for the dominant characteristics of Americanisation and nationalism respectively, as far as the supply of management books in Sweden is concerned. In the next chapter these two significant books are 'entered' in order to study the production of popular managerial manifestations in detail.

# 5 Popular management books as carriers of ideology

## Introduction[1]

As shown in the previous chapter, the vast majority of management books available in Sweden originate in either Sweden or the US. This could be interpreted as there being two parallel general trends in the international managerial discourse: nationalism and Americanisation. Furthermore, this pattern tends to be more marked the more popular and practically oriented the distribution channel. In this chapter we are going to examine two texts that represent these two general trends. The purpose is to discover whether they represent knowledge or ideology. In the previous chapter a comparison of data from different distribution channels showed one American title (*In Search of Excellence*) and one Swedish (*Service Management*) to be particularly significant to the Swedish discourse on management in the 1980s. These books are therefore selected for a detailed study of the production of popular managerial manifestations.[2] Two major strategies are used: to examine the texts, and to study the context in which they have been produced. In this chapter we employ the first strategy, while the latter will be employed in the following chapter.[3]

We shall examine the texts in three steps. First, the texts will be characterised in terms of their backgrounds, main issues and rhetorical characteristics. Second, we shall deconstruct their 'surface', i.e. analyse the underlying beliefs concerning issues like leadership, organisations and environments; these underlying discourses will serve as a deconstructive strategy, a point of departure for analysing the hidden agenda of management in the texts. The third step uses the findings of the first and second to discern what the texts represent as elements of the organisational environment in terms of two ideal types: knowledge and ideology.

The structure of the chapter is as follows. First the backgrounds to the texts are compared, and the main issues are discussed. Second, the books' rhetoric is examined and a deconstructive analysis performed. Finally, the characterisation of the two selected books in terms of knowledge or ideology is discussed.

## The background of the texts

*In Search of Excellence* (Peters and Waterman 1982) was written by two Americans, while *Service Management* (Normann 1983) is the work of a Swede who has lived in France since 1977 but spends much of his time in Sweden. All these authors hold doctorates and have long acted as management consultants. As will be discussed more thoroughly in the next chapter, Richard Normann has also worked in academia and was, for example, a professor at Lund University from 1984 to 1988.

The American authors worked for the American consulting firm McKinsey and Co., which operates worldwide, when they wrote their book. The book results from their assignment at McKinsey to a project on organisational effectiveness. It is based on interviews with their colleagues at McKinsey; documents on large, successful, and long-established companies and their founders; and the authors' personal experiences as consultants. Empirical data were collected mainly from successful companies chosen in order of profit in absolute numbers (based on the *Fortune* top 500 list).

Normann's book is the product of a similar process; it was initiated as a multi-client project to develop knowledge on service organisations when he was employed in one of the largest management consulting firms in Sweden at the time, SIAR (Scandinavian Institute of Administrative Research). The book was published after he had founded his own consulting firm SMG (Service Management Group, now SIFO Management Group) in 1980, and has been a core element in their consulting services ever since. He also writes in the preface that his ideas were influenced by the works on service organisations done at Harvard and in France, and also mentions some scholars by name (e.g. Chris Argyris, Michel Crozier, Pierre Eiglier, Eric Langaard, and Eric Rhenman – the latter was the founder of SIAR). All of them are in various ways associated with the activities of SIAR or SMG. Peters and Waterman make similar references, particularly to colleagues at McKinsey. Thus the empirical data and arguments in *Service Management* are primarily based on the author's and his colleagues' experiences from Scandinavian and a few French companies. However, examples from well known, successful American companies are used as well.

To conclude, the backgrounds of the texts display an almost identical pattern. All authors had been involved in academic research, the books were written in the context of consulting firms, and the data were based mainly on personal experiences and aggregate experiences from the consulting firms in which they were active.

## The main issues

*In Search of Excellence* was first published in 1982, and the main ambition of the book is to indicate characteristics which make some companies more successful than others.[4] The authors call such companies 'excellent', and their intentions are to define the meaning of 'excellence' and to explain what excellent companies do that others do not. They argue that all the most successful (excellent) American companies manifest eight attributes which they therefore claim to be 'the key to success'. The book is structured to show why these eight attributes of 'excellence' lead to success.

The attributes are:

1   'a bias for action', i.e. it is better to perform any action than none at all; action is a key to success;
2   'close to the customer' – it is the customers who pay the bills, therefore you must produce what they want to pay for;
3   'autonomy and entrepreneurship' – give all employees freedom and encourage them to improve their working routines and their products, as they know their own business best;
4   'productivity through people' – respect individual employees, make them into winners, let them excel and treat them as adults;
5   'hands-on, value-driven' – show personal attention to individuals at all levels of the organisation. In this way people should be motivated and thereby work better;
6   'stick to the knitting' – do not do what you are not good at; concentrate your efforts on what you know;
7   'simple form, lean staff' – avoid complex structures, stick to a divisionalised structure based on differences in products, and ensure communication throughout the organisation to let the basic values colour all activities;
8   'simultaneous loose-tight properties' – there must be rules of quality, service, innovations and experiments. But they should be based on the notion of expansion, not restriction.

The tenets which govern the major conclusions are that all excellent corporations have strong basic values such as:

> a belief in being the best; a belief in the importance of the details of execution, the nuts and bolts of doing the job well; a belief in the importance of people as individuals; a belief in superior quality and service; a belief that most members of the organization should be innovators, balanced by the willingness to support failure; a belief in the importance of informality to enhance communication; explicit belief in and recognition of the importance of economic growth and profits.
>
> (Peters and Waterman 1982: 285)

Excellent companies pursue these principles because they have effective leaders who create a system of values which is manifested.

An effective, successful leader is one who can arouse and maintain enthusiasm among employees (*ibid.*: 287). Only an effective leader has the ability to assemble individual values into a strong corporate culture. The great managers of 'excellent' companies act similarly in order to assemble, establish or convert values. The authors write that many leaders of the excellent corporations use open office doors as a symbol of encouragement of communication, and walk around to show their interest and involvement in what every single employee does. All these activities resulted in a creative, competent and motivated 'crew' in every 'excellent' company which carries out effective, innovative, qualitative and competitive work. According to Peters and Waterman, the top managers of the excellent companies always have this in mind, to create, maintain, diffuse and explain the value system of the company. They admit that it is not easy. The key is to persevere, to travel widely, and to work many hours of overtime, otherwise 'not much happens, it seems' (*ibid.*: 291).

The main issues in *Service Management* (Normann 1983) resemble those in *In Search of Excellence*.[5] Nevertheless, Normann presents a more specific model and concentrates chiefly on companies in the service industry. He writes that this industry is growing in modern western societies and defines what distinguishes service from manufacturing companies. The purpose of the book is to instruct executives in 'business management' on how they can increase their profit and their ability to grow. He focuses on how service organisations work and how they should be run in order to be 'good' (Normann 1983; 1991: 26). Unlike the authors of the American book he does not discuss culture in general as a new way of explaining what kinds of behaviour can be classed as excellent. Normann is more specific and presents a model which he claims can be used to diagnose the crucial factors of success in service organisations. Further, he comments on the need to discover how these factors can be reflected in the management's behaviour and in the organisation's culture, in order to create a system which can first be reproduced, and then maintained for a long period (*ibid.*: 65). Since he is concerned with a specific service management system, he uses terms other than culture and values in his arguments (e.g. image, philosophy, ideas, harmony). Nevertheless, in his two closing chapters he expounds on the general underlying thoughts behind his model and thereby refers to the organisational culture, sets of values, and the need and ability of management to control the culture (*ibid.*: 197). Earlier in the book he also writes that an important aspect of management consists in the ability to identify critical factors in the culture and create powerful ways to control and maintain them. In this respect he claims that the guiding principles are values, culture and ethical norms; and that there are no other ways to sustain high quality in the performance of every single employee than to maintain a thorough culture and to ensure that they not only have the right skills and competence but also are guided by the right ethical norms (*ibid.*: 63). Some values which the author mentions, and indeed reiterates from time to time, are orientation to the customer, attention to and education of employees, and effective leadership as the core of the culture. When he discusses the philosophy of good service organisations he also mentions the importance of values such as 'small is beautiful on a large scale', and 'strong focus but broad perspectives' (*ibid.*: 199).

The structure of the book follows a model called the Service Management System. This consists of two main systems: one for delivery of service, and one for harmony between different ideas (i.e. ideas for the staff, and ideas for business and organisation). The former system includes segmentation of the market and definition of customers, environment and technologies, qualities, and physical deliveries of peripheral and principal services. The second system includes the division of ideas for employment, individual development, education, strategy and policies, business, image, philosophy, culture, and leadership. Success will ensue if the system is in harmony and all its parts emanate from a few dominant ideas. In the book, the author deals with each item separately, but behind each part of the system there must be a strong culture and a number of values which colour what the company does. He writes: 'in order to be successful, a service company has to have an outstanding and consistent set-up of basic principles leaving marks on the organisation as a whole, from top to bottom through all levels in the moment of truth' (Normann 1984: 171). Furthermore, he argues that organisations need a few basic 'set-ups' and a strong corporate culture. This thesis pervades the book, although it is not discussed explicitly until one of the closing chapters. He also suggests that cultures evolve over time and that through 'effective, healthy, and valid values and beliefs' management can be seen as 'sources' of the culture in organisations. This growth process can be guided by the philosophy which is used to influence the corporate culture. The philosophy itself can be governed by the entire service management system, which must nevertheless be perfected by leaders and styles of leadership; these in turn can be controlled through norms, values, rules of play, role models and examination of individuals, all of which may be determined by the management. Here it is crucial that the management is visible and consistent if it is to be perceived as trustworthy. Otherwise the organisation runs the risk of entrapment in 'bad' circles instead of 'good'.[6]

## *Similarities and differences between the main issues*

To summarise the principal contents of the two books, it is obvious that the main issues circle around what can be characterised as identical labels, namely that companies will be successful if they have strong corporate culture, shared values, and effective leaders. The American authors also claim in their book that there is a need for a new theory and entrepreneurship as the key to successful evolution. However, there are also differences. Normann, for instance, does not argue in terms of corporate culture until the end of the book. His argument is thereby more stringent, more specific and less general as he explains his model in greater detail. He has simply used other terms besides 'culture', such as 'ideas for individuals' and 'delivery of services', or 'company image' and 'philosophy'. Nevertheless, behind his model we find that the main issues are similar to those stressed in the American book. The arguments which describe the attributes which make companies excellent are similar in both books, and in this case it does not matter whether the authors be from the US or from Sweden.

So at this level we can talk in terms of homogenisation rather than divergence between the two books, although they represent two general trends in the discourse. This also means that the two major trends in the Swedish discourse, nationalism and Americanisation, do not really differ in terms of topics and main issues discussed. Although not studied empirically here, there are reasons to believe that the same tendencies are to be found in popular books with origins other than Swedish. Next we consider the rhetoric of the each book to see if a deeper examination of the texts shows a similar or a different pattern.

## An analysis of the rhetoric used in the books

### *Fragmentary accounts as 'metaphors'*

One rhetorical device prominent in both books is that the authors often present their empirical observations as fragmentary narratives from a variety of successful, well known companies. In the American book these accounts regularly deal with questions concerning the behaviour of famous managers (often the founders of successful companies) or how the companies have made spectacular moves or turnarounds (the latter aspect also occurs in the Swedish book). *Service Management* takes its examples, naturally enough, from organisations in Sweden and France, although references to large, well known American companies such as McDonald's, Delta Airlines and IBM, which are used by Peters and Waterman as well, also feature in Normann's work. These narratives often take the form of glimpses of how successful companies handle certain situations, and are used by the authors as 'metaphors' to emphasise their points and lend credibility to their arguments. In what follows, a quotation from each book is selected to illustrate their setting in the texts. The first is from Peters and Waterman (1982: 233):

> At 3M, suppose someone working in the product development group in a division comes up with an idea. He first does the normal: he goes to his boss to seek funding. Suppose his boss turns him down. Then the 3M magic starts. He goes to another division within his group. If he's turned down again, he goes next to another division within his group. He may be in the adhesives group, but it's not unusual for him to wander over to office products. Now, if that group or some other doesn't have time for him, he goes to the court of last resort: NBVD. That's where the really far-out stuff ends up.
>
> How does 3M make an approach like this work? Simple: managers are given every incentive to do so. The fellow heading any group gets rewarded in part on the dollar amount of venture activity that he's funded from outside his group.

This account from Peters and Waterman's text exemplifies the importance for an organisation of having a culture which encourages innovators. In particular it appears as an account of how the management system at 3M provides incentives to managers and employees to be innovative and to try every possible way of obtaining funding for an idea. However, not much more additional information on the procedures for development of new products in 3M than is presented in the quotation is served to the reader. Consequently the credibility of the account is difficult to control. It is thereby appropriate to define accounts used in this way in a text as 'metaphors', i.e. as illustrations of the point the authors want to make. The credibility of the account thereby draws upon 3M as a well known, successful company, not on detailed systematic exemplification of how the procedures behind the process summarised in the account work. This way of building arguments is very common throughout Peters and Waterman's book.

A similar feature is also prominent in Normann's book. However, he is more moderate in this regard, possibly because his book is about 180 pages shorter than Peters and Waterman's.[7] Another difference, probably due to Normann's more specific argumentation and the fact that he follows a model more stringently, is that the accounts are more focused on particular issues. However, this means that the accounts are often adapted to illustrate what the author wants to show, and they are of a similar nature in both Normann's and Peters and Waterman's text. To illustrate their setting in the text, we have selected an account which appears when Normann discusses the need for internal marketing in organisations (Normann 1984: 114).

> When Jan Carlzon became the new chief executive of the ailing Scandinavian Airlines System, the fame of the company and various novel ideas about management which he immediately expressed made him a popular target for journalists. The innumerable articles about him in the mass media seem to have been studied more thoroughly by his staff than equivalent articles in internal publications would ever have been. Moreover, they drew SAS employees into discussing the company and the new interesting management ideas with people outside SAS. In many cases this has obviously served as a source for reinforcement, whereby employees have crystallized and internalized the ideas more strongly after having a chance to defend them against the world outside.

Here it can be seen how Normann reports that the attention which SAS, and especially the managing director Jan Carlzon, attracted in the press had an internal impact on SAS. He maintains that SAS was 'sick' before Carlzon was brought in, and that the new management ideas implemented thereafter caused a turnaround which made SAS 'healthy'. This turnaround also made Carlzon a popular figure with journalists, and Normann infers that this public interest caused the employees to be more receptive to the new, more service-oriented ideas. This account is thereby used by Normann to mark the importance of internal marketing as an element in the service management system. This feature is characteristic of Normann's text, whereby accounts similar to that discussed here are used as 'metaphors' to mark the point he wants to make.

Even though this kind of 'metaphoric' argumentation is prominent in both books, there is a difference in the use of their accounts. Normann's accounts tend to be adjusted to specific issues, while Peters and Waterman's are often more thrilling and related to extraordinary situations. Another difference is that the American book quotes many accounts from several successful companies to emphasise the credibility of a feature, while Normann often uses the reverse approach, i.e. he starts with the specific feature, and then cites one or several examples to illustrate his meaning. Thus Normann seeks to prove his point afterwards, while the others begin with the examples. As we have stated, there are differences in how accounts are used as 'metaphors' in the two texts; however, the tendency is typical of both.

## Universalism

Another rhetorical characteristic especially prominent in the American book is that it reports on one company, and then adds accounts of other firms insofar as these show a similar pattern. The examples used are often well known and extraordinary, and can be from almost any industry. The authors do not distinguish between the circumstances in different industries, and if they have found a common feature they present it as evidence that this is one general key to excellence. The following quotation illustrates how this characteristic appears in the American text (Peters and Waterman 1982: 155).

> If you've got a major problem, bring the right people together and expect them to solve it. The 'right people' very often means senior people who 'don't have the time.' But they do, somehow, have the time at Digital, TI, HP, 3M, IBM, Dana, Flour, Emerson, Bechtel, McDonald's, Citibank, Boeing, Delta, *et al.*

We see in the quotation how well known, successful companies like Digital, Hewlett-Packard (HP), McDonald's, 3M, Citibank, Boeing and Delta (Airlines) are mentioned in the same sentence. In other words the authors believe that since, for example, two producers of technical office and computer equipment (Digital, HP), one of fast food (McDonald's), one of office products (3M), one bank (Citibank), one aircraft manufacturer (Boeing), and one airline (Delta) have something in common, this is evidence of the universal validity of their observation. This is an ubiquitous characteristic of Peters and Waterman's text.

Normann's text also has this tendency, even though the examples are collected mainly from service companies. However, sometimes he also draws attention to other more general examples, for example Atlas-Copco (industrial products), Avis (car rental), an anonymous insurance company, IKEA (designers and distributors of home furniture) and Scandinavian Airlines System. This is illustrated in the following quotation (Normann 1984: 109–11).

> In the Atlas Copco case the image emerges of a company which is more creative than its competitors. ... The Avis 'We try harder' message has another content. ... An industrial risk insurance company with which we once worked owed much of its success to the fact that it was able to convey the idea, which it could also support in practice that 'this company doesn't start to dispute among the ruins'. ... The Swedish company IKEA ... is a case in point. ... Another typical illustration is provided by the Scandinavian Airlines System.

The quotation is an aggregate of some two pages of running text, demonstrating that Normann is again more moderate in his argumentation. While Peters and Waterman covered almost the entire business world in one sentence, Normann takes two pages to discuss three examples. However, the tendency of the authors to make universal claims is still obvious in both books, even though it is a more marked characteristic of the American text. Besides, it is also fair to note that the American authors discuss excellence in general while Normann chiefly refers to 'good service companies' in the service industry.

### Personal expertise, normativity and positioning to other studies

Another rhetorical feature of the two books is that the argumentation is personal. The authors frequently argue in terms of 'We found', 'I saw', 'He said', 'Let us look at', etc. In this respect they present the findings as if they, or someone well known to them (a colleague or a friend) were involved. In other words they present data and observations in a personal way based on their own experiences. As noted above, there is a tendency in both texts to refer to observations of many different companies, and since they write in this personal way they present themselves (or their colleagues) as very experienced individuals who know what they are talking about. This is the most marked rhetorical device of both books. Again, to illustrate the setting of this feature, we shall select a quotation from each book.

In Peters and Waterman's book, one representative example of this feature is the following condensed extract, the first part of which, according to the authors, is a rough transcript of a chat between the authors and an old colleague who had recently started a chain of McDonald's restaurants in Switzerland. In the text the conversation 'took place one sunny, calm spring day in a canoe on the mirror waters of Lake Geneva' (Peters and Waterman 1982: xix). The man talked about his first impressions of McDonald's and gave the following comment (xix–xxii):

> You know, one of the things that strikes me most about McDonald's is their people orientation. During the seven years I was at McKinsey, I never saw a client that seemed to care so much about its people.

And Peters and Waterman continue:

> Another friend described for us why, in a recent major computer system purchase for a hospital, he chose International Business Machines ...
>
> In teaching workshops for clients or students, we often use a case built around Delta Airlines' unique management style. We who travel a lot are apt to tell a story or two about the material assistance we have gotten from Delta's gate employees while scrambling to make a last-minute connection. The last time we did it, one executive raised his hand and said: – Now let me tell you how it really is in Delta ...

And the stories go on. What really fascinated us as we began to pursue our survey of corporate excellence was that the more we dug, the more we realized the excellent companies abounded in such stories and imagery. We began to realize that these companies had cultures as strong as any Japanese organization.

As can be seen in the extract, the authors first draw upon a personal chat with a friend who, on the basis of his experiences with McKinsey and McDonald's, 'delivers' information which the reader should trust since he 'has been there' and knows what he is talking about. Moreover, they also 'deliver' information based on their own experiences from meetings with business people and as travellers with Delta.

When comparing this view with Normann's book the similarities are striking. It is difficult to find differences between the books, but again Normann is more moderate. In other words his argumentation is, as with the characteristics discussed above, more specific and focused on explaining elements in his model. To illustrate this feature we have selected two quotations from different parts of the book:

> When I recently visited a New York suburb, however, and asked for a Big Mac in a McDonald's at 9 o'clock in the morning, the employee was thoroughly startled and appeared to be completely flummoxed. Obviously the programming had never envisaged a customer so uneducated as not to know that McDonald's don't serve hamburgers for breakfast.
>
> (Normann 1984: 73)

> From personal experience and the study of successful organizations, I have identified a pattern of what seems to characterize the culture and management philosophies of successful, service-oriented business today. Observations of companies in many types of business, servicing a variety of customers, representing diverse service concepts and possessing different delivery systems and organisation structures have revealed a common pattern of culture and dominating ideas. Specifics may differ, but at a reasonable level of generalization these companies do share some fundamental ideas.
>
> Starting from these observations, which I admit have not been tested with scientific rigour, I hazard a tentative proposition: not only are the culture and normative guiding principles generally a crucial success factor and a distinguishing feature of any service organisation or knowledge-intensive business; there are also several specific and necessary ingredients in the culture of all such companies.
>
> (*ibid.*: 166)

As can be seen here, the notion that Normann has 'been there' is obvious. He has not only visited a McDonald's restaurant, he also writes categorically that he bases his conclusions on his personal experience, and that from this source he has identified patterns of what he believes are characteristics of the culture in many companies, and so on and so forth.

The text of both books can be described as subjective, since they often draw on personal experience and discoveries. This personal approach to an argument shows the author of the text as an expert: he (or someone in his group) has been there, and he (or someone in his group), or a close colleague or friend, has discovered what others have not, namely what kind of behaviour characterises good and excellent companies, and how to achieve and maintain this excellence over a long period.

Closely linked to the air of expertise stressed in the books is their pronounced normative character. Peters and Waterman claim that all the excellent companies are characterised by their attributes and that imitation of them will result in long-term success. Normann describes a system which can 'diagnose' the root of the problem in the service companies, and how this can be overcome if the whole service management system is in harmony.

The authors also refer to research in the field, and to articles in business magazines. These references are used in the same way as the various examples from different companies, namely to strengthen the arguments. However, their main frame of reference is primarily mentioned in the preface. It is interesting to note that Normann refers to Peters and Waterman's book, and that the latter cite a SIAR report on 'Management as statesmanship' written by Normann in 1976. Otherwise they have only two references in common, namely March and Simon (1958) and Toffler (1980). Moreover, Peters and Waterman draw on theoretical results in the literature and lead the reader through summaries and discussions of earlier work in this field. In this respect their book, rather than Normann's, can be seen as a medium for diffusion of 'established' organisation theory to a wider audience than the international academic community.

### Platitudes

Both books claim to be normative, and this yields another rhetorical device which they have in common. That is, in order to fulfil their ambition to be normative (to give answers), their arguments, as will be shown below, can often be characterised as consisting of a mass of statements and platitudes.

The appearance of platitudes in Peters and Waterman's text can be seen already in the title: *In Search of Excellence: Lessons from America's Best-run Companies*. They seek to present facts about successful companies, their reason being the statement that there is a causal relationship between the facts observed in 'excellent' companies and universal methods of achieving success. This is characteristic of the conclusions drawn in the book. In their preface, Peters and Waterman (1982: xv) comment on the eight attributes which, they claim, define excellence:

> Each finding in and of itself may seem like a platitude (close to the customers, productivity through people), but the intensity of the way in which the excellent companies execute the eight [findings] – especially when compared with their competitors – is as rare as a smog-free day in Los Angeles.

This passage indicates that the argument can often be characterised as categorical. The authors use a simile – which is also an undeniable fact – that 'a smog-free day in Los Angeles' is rare, to verify that 'excellent' companies are extraordinary. This feature recurs throughout the book, i.e. flat statements which make many of the conclusions seem so true as to be difficult to contradict. Let us consider another example (Peters and Waterman 1982: 156):

> The good news from the excellent companies is the extent to which, and the intensity with which, the customer intrudes into every nook and cranny of the business – sales, manufacturing, research, accounting. A simple message permeates the atmosphere. All business success rests on something labelled a sale, which at least momentarily weds company and customer. A simple summary of what our research uncovered on the customer attribute is this: the excellent companies really are close to their customers. That's it. Other companies talk about it; the excellent companies do it.

They state that excellent companies involve their customers in everything they do. Moreover, that the excellent companies' atmospheres are permeated by a notion of selling and that each sale is a contact between company and customer. In consequence they say that excellent companies really do have close contact with their customers, and that while other companies talk about this, the excellent companies practise it. Again we see how the authors add statements one after another and then, based thereon, they draw conclusions which therefore can be characterised as platitudes. The same rhetorical device also appears in *Service Management*; however, again, Normann is more moderate in his conclusions, as can be demonstrated by the following extract (Normann 1984: 43).

> The customer is not just an onlooker; his presence in this particular context creates a social dynamic which makes the employees conscious of their roles and their prestige, which in turn helps to create a genuine new experience and a sense of participation in the customer.
>
> In a well-designed service delivery system we will find that the employee, the client and any other organized but not employed participant all emerge from the process of service delivery and/or service consumption with an enhanced sense of self-esteem. They feel the better for it.

Normann remarks that the customer is not an onlooker, and then concludes that since the client participates, his presence creates a social dynamic which makes the employees conscious of their roles and gives them new experience and a notion of client participation. By adding another statement, that all individuals involved in good service delivery systems will enhance their self-esteem, he concludes that this is an effect of a well designed system. In this respect Normann's conclusions can be called platitudes, i.e. the complexity of defining a good service delivering system is excluded from the text and the reader must therefore rely on the author's statement. However, the fact that an argument can be characterised as consisting of statements and platitudes does not mean that it is wrong. It is only a classification of the author's rhetoric. It can be further illustrated by the following passage from the book (Normann 1984: 62–3):

> People in different social situations, at different stages of their lives and with different lifestyles have different needs, motivations and ambitions. They will mobilize their energy for the company only if the tasks and activities required by its business needs somehow fit their needs as individuals. And – even more interesting – this is a plus-sum game: by providing a suitable setting or context for the individual the company performs a service for him and, in many cases, also an important social function.

> This is part of the background to the common claim that serv-
> ice companies must market themselves not only to their clients
> but also to their employees.

This passage shows how Normann uses a generally accepted truth, that different people have different needs, to reach his conclusion that companies which supply a suitable framework both favour the individual, and benefit from mobilising his energy. In this respect another characteristic of Normann's text is that specific conclusions, such as the importance for service companies of working with internal marketing, is based upon general truths. However, it could also be argued that he sets his specific conclusions in a broader perspective. But in his text he tends to use the broad discussion to verify his specific conclusions, not the reverse, i.e. the specific findings are verified by certain selective evidence and arguments.

If we compare Peters and Waterman's accumulation of statements to draw their conclusions (characterised as platitudes) with Normann's arguments, the latter's more moderate style of making claims is obvious. He is not as broad and sweeping as the American authors, but nevertheless is not so specific as to support his arguments by introducing the reader to their origin or other work on the topic. This means that the reader is left to rely on the author's expertise. Unless he is an expert him/herself, the reader has few opportunities to go deeper and to read more on specific discussions, or to check whether the author really is such an expert as his text presents him to be.

## Labels

It has been said above that Normann's book is more specific than Peters and Waterman's. This becomes even more noticeable if we consider the occurrence of 'labels'. However, there are other differences as well. The American authors tend to use the main issues identified above – strong corporate culture, shared values and strong leaders – as labels in their texts, so that they almost take the meaning of these words for granted. They use many examples, which were defined above as often metaphorical, but they do not give a clear explanation of what, for instance, the word 'strong' means when they talk about culture, or what 'effective' means when they talk about leadership. They merely say that strength and effectiveness are synonymous with powerful, and usually mean that less excellent companies do not have a strong culture, effective leaders, or shared values. Thus the most important elements of their argument, the main issues (strong culture, shared values and effective leadership) are used as labels for processes which they do not properly define. Their discussions thereby become vague, unspecified, and commonplace in the sense that they are hard to deny since the definitions are so general and so broad. Normann's rhetoric is in this respect more specific, since the main issues are hidden behind his rigid model of the service management system. When he discusses his model he explains every detail extensively, and at the end of the book, when he focuses on the basic questions behind his system, he relates such terms as culture, values and leadership to his earlier arguments in a deductive way. Normann is thereby more stringent when he uses different terms. His model does consist of a set of labels, but he makes efforts to explain them to a greater extent than do Peters and Waterman.

### Concluding remarks on similarities and differences in rhetoric

In conclusion, we could say that there are some virtually identical rhetorical characteristics in both books, even though *Service Management* diverges in some respects and reveals a more moderate style. For instance, it was observed that both books make frequent use of metaphors in combination with platitudes, normativity and personal expertise. It is true that these rhetorical devices appear in different ways in each book, i.e. even though both books display these features this is not to say that they are used in the same context. Nevertheless, it is obvious that this writing technique, i.e. the use of these rhetorical instruments, is characteristic of both texts. Another feature common to both books is that the authors reiterate that their observations are based on long experience; they tend to draw upon their personal expertise to make their arguments credible. This is probably the most marked similarity of the rhetoric in these texts. In fact we could almost call them identical in this regard.

However, there are also differences in the books' use of rhetoric. Regarding the use of labels, for instance, only a few were observed in Normann's book. This is probably a consequence of his more moderate style throughout, where his claims and arguments tend to be more specific and designed to explain the concepts of his model (the service management system). Another difference pertains to claims for universal validity, where the American book tends to be more marked since the authors do not distinguish between different industries. The Swedish book, on the other hand, is mainly focused on service organisations, even though the defining limits for such organisations seem to be fairly wide. Nevertheless, Peters and Waterman also explicitly relate their arguments to the results of others, so their book thereby can be said to score higher in respect of positioning to other studies. Normann's text lacks such an explicit discussion. His arguments use many references, but these serve to strengthen his empirical findings. In this respect it can hardly be seen as a positioning to other studies.

To conclude, the rhetoric in the two books is similar in some respects and different in others. However, it seems that there is more in the rhetoric to unite the books than divide them, especially when it comes to the principal rhetorical features of each. So, not even in terms of rhetoric do we find any remarkable differences between American books and those produced domestically.

## Deconstruction of the texts: the search for a hidden agenda

Hitherto the two books in focus appear to be similar in terms of the backgrounds of the texts, the main issues and the rhetoric, even though differences can be observed regarding how they emphasise certain claims and aspects. The above analyses were mainly carried out in an ethnographic mode whereby one aspect at a time was analysed (e.g. Kets de Vries and Miller 1987; Czarniawska-Joerges 1988). In this section we continue the analysis of the books; and starting with the conclusions from the above analyses we shall compare the texts with something else. We thereby use a deconstructive strategy, or what Cooper (1988) describes as a decomposition of the surface, to study what Latour (1987) calls the hidden agenda.

The theme of both books deals with how management, by using the culture as a tool, can lead their organisations to success. In 'telling' this story, the authors use two leading actors, the manager and the managed, while the scenario is the organisation. The plot cannot be defined as comedy, tragedy or thriller; it is rather a drama of the social realism of interaction between individuals where the manager plays the principal part. This means that important elements of the argument in the texts may be seen as discussions around concepts like 'leadership' and 'organisations' and how they are related to their environments. Since these two discussions hold sway, it seems appropriate to depart from them when we deconstruct the texts to search for a hidden agenda. So, by using these concepts as a deconstructive strategy it is possible, as Cooper (1988) suggests, to determine the assumptions on which the arguments in the texts rest.

## Leadership

When good managers are discussed in the two books, a significant attribute consists of their ability to perform symbolic actions which allude to the basic values in the culture. In this way the 'good' leader expresses values which are recalled by the employees in their daily actions. Symbolism is thereby mentioned as one of the secrets of strong leadership. Thus the authors suggest that the leader controls the organisation by creating and maintaining norms and values which are expressed in words, texts or symbolic gestures related to incentives and contributions, communication, education, slogans and policies, and information about overall goals. The organisation's destiny is in the hands of the leader, as he (for the leader appears as a 'he' rather than a 'she') has the ability, provided he is effective, to create a strong culture which will enable the organisation to be successful. If the opposite is true – if he is ineffective – subcultures working in their own interest, not the organisation's, may become established, which will lead to the organisation's failure.

This view of symbolic actions differs from Pfeffer's discussion from 1981, where managerial actions may have symbolic meanings while this need not be the manager's intention. In Pfeffer's view it might very well happen that the leader speaks of strategies, plans and objectives for the company, but the influence of his words may be symbolic rather than actual (see also Brunsson 1989). In the books analysed, however, both intentions and actions are likely to be seen as rational (i.e. means-end relationships) and can be controlled by the leader himself.

The classical view of leadership (cf. Fayol 1916; 1949; Taylor 1911) is that the manager is mainly presented as a conductor, i.e. he supervises all activities of the organisation just as a conductor leads his orchestra. This means that the leader should fulfil the requirements of POSDCORB – Planning, Organising, Staffing, Directing, CoOrdinating, Reporting, Budgeting (Gulick *et al.* 1937). If we examine what the books say about leadership, this does indeed differ from the classical view of how an orchestra should be conducted. However, they still see the leader as a conductor, but not one who compels every single individual to play every note in the score. They rather see him as the one who ensures that all members of the orchestra play in the same key and follow the same harmonies. He also explains to them the meaning of learning to play the notes, but he does not conduct them when they play; he expects them to understand why they should play according to what is written in the score. What the authors say is that if he practises with strength this type of control, the organisation will become successful. There it is again – strength! What do they mean by strength?

It is said that an effective leader expresses the values of the culture so clearly that all employees, in all of their daily routines, act with the organisation's values as point of departure. Furthermore, that good managers, by making symbolic moves, i.e. rewarding 'right' and 'heroic' behaviour, create a system where employees apply the 'right' values and learn what kind of behaviour is right and therefore rewarded, and what behaviour is wrong and therefore not rewarded. Thus by good management they mean successful manipulation. In this respect, the behaviour of a successful leader resembles that of a good animal tamer, who uses different rewards to encourage his or her animals to do what is required. Attributes associated with a tamer seem to be related to what the authors mean by 'strength', insofar as they claim that successful leadership emanates from the leaders' ability to induce employees to work for the overall goals of the organisation by publishing slogans, setting values and norms, establishing obvious relations between incentives and contributions, and achieving clarity in symbolic actions. The authors imply that a leader should show which values and norms will be rewarded in the organisation.

The point is that by so doing, the leader creates a system of what Perrow (1986) discussing Barnard's work (1938), calls 'unobtrusive control'. In this regard it is fairly obvious that the representations of the leader in the books are related to Barnard's ideas whereby top managers make the overall decisions about strategies, policies, leadership styles, etc. and control employees by instilling basic values through 'manipulative' strategies. According to this view of the leader, he controls the organisation through motivated employees whom he enlists through 'indoctrination', 'manipulation' and an obvious connection between incentives and contributions. Again we concur with the view of the leader as suggested by Barnard (1938).

Peters and Waterman's and Normann's leader is proactive and knows how to play his cards right in order to induce his employees to make the 'right' moves. In this respect he expresses very clearly whither the company is bound and how to get there. However, if we examine studies which follow managers in their daily work, they are likened to a 'puppet in a puppet show' rather than a 'conductor standing aloof on his platform' (Carlzon 1951; 1991: 46; see also Stewart 1967: 88; Mintzberg 1973). This means that he pays attention to what is happening at the moment rather than supervising overall activities. The leader presented in these studies reacts. This point is not raised in the analysed texts. Peters and Waterman mention Mintzberg's study but do not dwell on the discussion therein.

Consequently, neither book questions the leader's proactive role in a company's evolution or success. In other words, the authors do not discuss, or even mention, views which do not glorify the leader. They (the Americans in particular) claim to present an alternative to classical rational leadership models, but arrive at another, rational (means-end) view with strong roots in Barnard's 1938 argument, where top management takes all the important decisions and 'manipulates' employees into acquiescence. It is not a view wherein the manager controls the organisation by job specialisation and direct supervision. Their rational alternative is that the manager should express the company's vision, mission and overall goals very clearly, and create a system to manipulate and indoctrinate employees into learning these tenets and the basic values which will guide them, and thereby the organisation, to these goals. Thus both books appear to claim that the top management comprises those who know, and therefore those who should guide and decide which direction and what behaviour and what goals, values, etc. are right and wrong for the company.

## Organisations and environments

It was stated above that according to the view of leadership in the books under discussion, an organisation is expected to be a tool whereby an effective management can realise its visions and overall goals. Thus they do not advocate a classical bureaucratic system, but an informal one, since it does not consist of rules and job descriptions. Instead it is supposed to be defined at a 'paradigmatic level' where every individual should understand what he or she is doing and why (cf. Barnard 1938). This view of an organisation seems to derive from the notion that it is possible to clearly distinguish between internal and external activities. In this respect the authors can be considered to believe in the possibilities of protecting the internal system from environmental influence provided the company has a 'strong' corporate culture. Nevertheless the authors do not express it in these terms; they seem to advocate a closed system (cf. Thompson 1967).

Considerations of only the 'surface' of the texts, i.e. what the authors suggest in their own words, conveys the impression that they would prefer the organisation to be an open system with a large capacity for flexibility. The openness they suggest, however, seems mainly to concern close relations in general and flexibility only towards the customers. All other aspects (internal or external, like suppliers or competitors) are supposed to be controlled by effective leadership. In this regard it seems that the organisation should be protected from all influences save those of the management and the customers.

The conclusion that leaders must act effectively seems to imply that leadership is a political process and that organisations are political systems (Pfeffer and Salancick 1978; Morgan 1986). Both books mention that coalitions other than management can sometimes become powerful (e.g. Cyert and March 1963), but if the management is aware of this, they need simply to act more forcefully to attain their ends. It is obvious that the authors see politics as one of the principal aspects of leadership and of how organisations work, though this remains implicit. Furthermore, it is clear that they nearly always regard management as the most powerful coalition in good organisations. This is connected with the discussion of enactment of reality. Both books discuss the necessity of demonstrating which values and activities in the organisation are rewarded. It would seem that the authors see the leader as a constructor of the organisational view of reality, whose job it is to communicate this view to the employees. The authors mention that there may also be others in the organisation who communicate views of realities, but they seldom see this as problematic since the manager, if he is effective, is still the chief constructor of reality. In this way the authors cite discussions by Selznick (1957), Berger and Luckmann (1967) and Weick (1979a) of the social construction of reality, but they neglect the unforeseen, the unplanned, the unintended.

The above discussion suggests that adjustment to the environment is only meant to happen in regard to the customers, and that the definition of organisations is related to classical theories where organisations can, allegedly, be protected from all external influences save the customers'. Rather, the organisational political system is supposed to give the power to indoctrinate and control employees' enactment of reality to the leader, but only if he is effective (cf. Barnard 1938). However, it is not a classical bureaucratic system of rules which is suggested, but rather an indoctrinative system of ideas, where freedom of thought is fine, but only if the thinking is right!

## Conclusions: the hidden agenda

The analysis made in this section has indicated that the hidden agendas of both texts seem to be almost homogeneous. In other words, no particular differences were found in the deconstructive analyses of the texts in terms of leadership, and organisations and environments.

This is interesting, since the books were produced in different contexts, i.e. the US and Sweden. The view of the hidden agenda which both books seem to have in common can be presented as in the concluding summary below. However, it is worthy of note that this is a summary of the discussions above, not a summary of the overt arguments used by Peters and Waterman and Normann themselves.

Good top managers are omnipotent and can, due to their ability to diagnose the company's situation, create values and overall goals which will lead the organisation to success if the employees follow them (however, in this process they may sometimes need the help of external consultants). To ensure that employees do the right things, the leader should act as a tamer and teach, manipulate and indoctrinate his staff in the right values, norms, morals, ideologies, etc. In this regard the right ones lead to success and therefore should represent points of departure for individuals in their performance of organisational activities. This means that individuals need to be supervised, otherwise they can grasp the 'wrong' enactments and their performance will be of less benefit to the organisation. If the individuals understand the meaning of their work, they will be satisfied and more motivated to fulfil their duties, and the organisation will thereby become efficient. Linked to this is the point that the organisation must be flexible with respect to its customers, but closed against other environmental elements. The leader controls the whole system with openness to customers and exclusion of other environmental elements by political power where he acts as a statesman. The key to success is that the political system actually gives all power to the leader, if he is strong. Thus the leader creates the culture, values and management styles of the organisation. This means that the organisation is a social construction which is created among the individuals. Further, the individuals' places and tasks in the organisation, and how they should interact and cooperate with their colleagues and customers, are decided and explained by the leader. If the leader is effective the individuals will understand their role, if he is not, the organisation will fail.

This summary implies that the view of management which emerges here resembles that of Barnard (1938) when he discusses how organisations work and how leadership should be practised; especially in the sense that the manager is the protagonist when successful decisions and plans for the future, are to be made. One of Barnard's points was that organisations' performance would be more efficient if the employees understood how their individual efforts contribute to first the group's and then the organisation's total output. He felt that the task of management was to decide what the organisation should do, then somehow to induce employees to work as efficiently as possible. In this regard he suggested both clear rewards for individual contributions, and articulations of slogans and policies to encourage staff and inform them of the organisations' overall goal and task. The clue was motivation inasmuch as motivated employees work more efficiently. Behind such a view lies the belief that the management knows best and that organisational success depends on its ability to discern the right direction for the organisation and then to design a structure and atmosphere in which the employees can see this direction and are encouraged and motivated to follow it. Behind such a view lie rational assumptions that something in general is right or wrong and that good leaders will know what is right and thereby best for the company. In other words the authors (i.e. Peters and Waterman and Normann) seem to take for granted that organisations become successful through effective leadership and management. This seems to be the foundation of both books, so that no alternative explanations are tested, e.g. that the products and services offered by companies regarded by the authors as successful may satisfy popular demand. Moreover, they do not discuss the possibility that unsuccessful organisations also may practise similar procedures and systems of management. Consequently, there is a clear tendency in both books to avoid and neglect explanations of why some organisations succeed which do not glorify the importance of management. To conclude, it therefore seems fair to say that the basic tenet of both books, and also their underlying message, is that there are rational correlations between the actions of management and the success of organisations. The right way to do this is, as argued above, for the organisation to be close to the customers, and 'protected' by management from other influences in society.

## What do the texts represent: knowledge or ideology?

So far the comparison of *In Search of Excellence* and *Service Management* has revealed a homogenisation in regard to the background of the texts, minor differences in rhetorical characteristics, and uniformity in the underlying arguments, i.e. the hidden agenda. But the question remains: what do such texts represent as elements of the organisational environment? Can they be characterised as representing knowledge or ideology? In order to answer this we here use the concepts of knowledge, beliefs, myths, institutions and ideology. In particular, as dealt with more thoroughly in the Appendix to this book, we concentrate on the argument for the underlying ideas in the texts, not the ideas as such. In other words, can the argument be said to have a cognitive rhetoric, or is it better described as ideological? The question of how the texts, as representing either knowledge or ideology, are related to institutional mechanisms in the organisational environment and thereby organisational identity, structure, and activities (cf. Meyer 1994) is discussed in the closing chapter of this study, which deals with the relation between discourse and consumption of representations thereof (such as books) in organisations.

As pointed out above in the analysis of the books' rhetoric, it was observed that the authors tended to use references and their own experiences as evidence to strengthen their conclusions. In a sense this can be seen as positioning, since they do indicate the traditions of thought which they draw on, but they do not clarify what they argue against. In other words, references to other relevant studies appear, but primarily to discussions which support the notions the authors advocate.

Another similar feature is that other studies can be used as references to show the failure of management. An obvious example of this is when Peters and Waterman (1982: 6–7) discuss Weick's (1979), March's (e.g. March and Olsen 1976) and Mintzberg's (1973) criticism of the rational perspective on management. These researchers state that organisational developments can be described as learning and adaptation processes, where solutions and problems emanating from previous experience are likely to be adopted in certain situations, and that managers mainly react to problems, rather than take the initiative in order to create great plans and strategies. Peters and Waterman maintain that these authors identify characteristics of ineffective management, i.e. managerial failures, and use these studies as evidence that excellent organisations do not suffer from such. Instead, they are more likely to be characterised by effective leadership. Normann makes similar use of references, although chiefly in support of his points. Thus he is more precise and does not distort their meaning as do Peters and Waterman. However, one conclusion which can be drawn from this is that the two books in focus do not really discuss the findings of others, or 'cross other people's paths' (Latour 1987) in reaching their results. That is, they do not elaborate on the references they use; they are more likely to adduce them as evidence. This means that they do not contradict these studies in their argument. So, the introduction of references into the argument can be described by saying that the authors take paths travelled by others, but that these paths do not lead to studies which do not support the points the authors want to make. But if they should do, as in the example from Peters and Waterman above, they twist the conclusion drawn in them and use them as evidence to support the stability of their own argument. This is typical of the two books in focus for the present study, although it in one way or another may be the general practice of many scholars in social science and management studies.

Instead of a positioning to other studies, the authors have a tendency, as pointed out in the rhetorical analysis above, to draw upon their personal experience. In their presentation of data and reasons for conclusions, instead of relating their findings to other studies or to methodological restrictions, they base their arguments on myths of what successful managers and companies do. These appear in the texts as examples of 'good' or successful managerial behaviour and organisation. By the same token the authors also refer to their own experience of consultancy assignments and meetings with successful managers and organisations.

In this regard the texts can be characterised as personal, i.e. the argument does not seek to be regarded as 'objective', i.e. to deal with impersonal 'facts'. This suggests a paradox, since the authors also have normative and universal ambitions (even though Normann's text is focused on organisations in the service industry). Consequently, judgements of the credibility of the argument are left to how much the reader believes in the authors' expertise and authority. If the reader is sceptical of this, then it is also easy to be sceptical about the authors' conclusions. That is, the high degree of personal expertise in the rhetoric detracts from the objectivity of the text and limits the ability of a reader to control the sources and read supportive (or non-supportive) studies of similar processes. Consequently, the credibility of the conclusions is weak (i.e. not stable or mobile) when the arguments are combined with other studies, since the authors have based their arguments mainly on their personal experience.

Further, when the texts were deconstructed it was indicated that both books seemed to be based on the same premise, i.e. that the organisation is a tool for the manager, if he is effective, to establish therein the right visions, morality and values, which staff will then have as the basis of their behaviour. They will also make the 'right' moves. In this way the organisation is expected to be successful, but must also be flexible to its customers. That this is the core of management and the right view of how organisations work is not easy to prove. But since all books can be described as normative, the authors claim to offer the right model. However, since it is a difficult task to prove, i.e. to present unambiguous conclusions, the authors use statements, institutionalised myths and beliefs, saying for example that the key to long-term organisational success is the omnipotence of the management in general and the managing director in particular. The conclusions of both books are founded on this notion of management. Clearly, this is taken for granted, i.e. its validity is not discussed or questioned. This means that this notion can be regarded as established, as a particular institution of management. Due to the uniformity of a Swedish and an American book created independently of each other, this institution could be interpreted as an indication of a general tendency in the modern western world.

Following from the discussions above, it seems that the label 'knowledge', i.e. that the argumentation should be stable, mobile, and combinable (cf. Latour 1987) does not apply to these texts. Thus the arguments are definitely not so loosely coupled that we should speak of free association (Weick 1979a). Instead the argumentation in both books is based on references to well established studies, myths from well known successful managers and organisations, and the personal experience of the authors and their colleagues. In this way they develop normative arguments regarding the operations of management and organisations which are based on institutionalised notions that organisational success is a function of effective leadership.

Consequently, they could be defined as related to beliefs concerning how to attain an ideal reality, rather than to what we know about the complexities inherent in the creation of a collective ideal situation. In particular they can be seen as being founded on a mixture of knowledge, beliefs, myths, and institutions, composed as an ideal view of reality. In other words, they can be regarded as particular packages of normative explanations of how management and organisations work. In this regard they can be seen as attempts to make sense of the ambiguous world 'out there' (cf. Alvarez 1991: 48). This means that they constitute collections of concepts, and sets of values and beliefs concerning what reality would be if it were ideal (cf. Berger and Luckmann 1967: 70; Alvesson and Berg 1988: 70). In this respect 'ideological' seems to be an appropriate label for the arguments in these books.

## Conclusions

This chapter has demonstrated that the backgrounds of *In Search of Excellence* and *Service Management* are similar. The same pattern was observed concerning the main issues. In the analysis of the rhetoric used in the two books, only minor differences were observed. Analyses of the texts' hidden agendas revealed a striking similarity where organisational success is taken for granted as a function of effective leadership. Finally, these observations have been discussed in order to describe the texts as representing either a cognitive or an ideological rhetoric. This discussion implied that they are ideological, since they can be broadly seen as personal declarations of the beliefs of the authors rather than arguments that are mobile and combinable.

The analyses in this chapter showed the texts to be similar in most of the aspects discussed. However, since the analyses were made chiefly in the ethnographic mode, i.e. no predestined model was followed, where the intention was to characterise the main issues, the rhetoric, the hidden agenda, and the possible representation of knowledge or ideology, the search was open and unspecified. This means that it may be difficult to identify differences between the books in this way. However, the reason why this study finds them to be similar may also be that they actually are similar in the aspects discussed here.

Consequently, since the books chosen here for detailed analyses represent the two trends of the general managerial discourse observed in the previous chapter, Americanization and nationalism, it can be argued that American perspectives dominate. The most significant difference between the books, as analysed here, is therefore their place of production and the nationality of the producers. The contents and the rhetoric, however, appear to be more or less identical.

# 6 How popular management books are made[1]

## Introduction

The tendency of North American management standards to dominate the popular managerial discourse is becoming more and more plain in this sudy. Thus the story told over and over again in popular management books is that the destiny of organisations is a function of the activities taken by their managers. Moreover, it appeared very clearly in Chapter 4 that the authors of books that achieve considerable popularity often happen to be consultants or successful managers.

In the previous chapter we examined two popular texts of particular significance in the Swedish managerial discourse of the 1980s. Here we take another grip on the discourse by examining the context in which one of these books was produced. The selected context is the same as that which produced the Swedish book analysed in the previous chapter, *Service Management* (1983) by the Swedish management consultant and Ph.D. Richard Normann. Due to the similarities between this book and its American counterpart (*In Search of Excellence*) analysed in Chapter 5, there are reasons to believe that the Swedish context is representative of environments where this kind of books is produced. The story told here can thereby be seen as an illustration of the kind of environment or 'laboratory' where many popular management books are made. *Service Management* was published in 1983, but may still be relevant when considering popular books of the late 1990s such as Hammer and Champy (1993) and Senge (1990). It will also be pertinent to our discussion of books authored by early gurus such as Taylor, Maslow and McGregor. The story told here can therefore be seen as an illustration of how popular management books are produced today, how they may previously have been produced, and how they will be produced in future.

By making an attempt to reconstruct the context which among other things resulted in *Service Management*, we here raise the question of why popular management books in the western world tend to end up conveying North American management standards. In this regard we will pay attention to the main reasons why popular books take a certain form and carry a certain content. Analyses are made in terms of the motives, considerations, social forces (cf. Latour 1987) and institutional mechanisms in society (cf. Meyer 1994) which contribute to the development of the context and thus the production of the texts. In so doing the aim is to attain a broader and more comprehensive view of what books such as those studied in the previous chapter represent as elements of the organisational environment.

## How *Service Management* was produced

The process which resulted in *Service Management* took place in the context of two management consulting firms, SIAR (Scandinavian Institute of Administrative Research, later SIAR-Bossard) and SMG (the Service Management Group, later SIFO Management Group) which Richard Normann founded in 1980 after leaving SIAR. This context has produced a number of books similar to *Service Management*. It was especially a feature in SIAR since the idea, at least in the early years, was that SIAR associates would combine consultation with academic research. This policy also gave space to the writing of textbooks and practically oriented handbooks on organisation theory and management. The analyses made here may therefore have a wider bearing than merely to represent the production of one particular book.

The data presented in this chapter were collected by interviews with eighteen respondents who were involved in SIAR's and SMG's development or who worked close to them. Data are also taken from secondary material like newspaper interviews with the founder of SIAR, advertising material from SMG, various publications about SIAR, and other books created in that context. The respondents were asked to tell their own story of the development of the two consulting firms, and the books were analysed in a similar way as in the previous chapter, although these analyses will not be presented in detail here while still being used as complementary data. These stories have then been analysed and interpreted.

The structure of the chapter is as follows: first, we recount the development of the context, from the foundation of SIAR in the mid-1960s to the early 1990s. This is followed by discussions of the institutional circumstances that surrounded the context. Here we will focus on both external and internal forces acting on the organisation. Then, internal motives and considerations will be examined.

## From research institute to consulting firm

As stated in the previous chapter, the particular process which led to the publication of *Service Management* began six years earlier in 1977 as a multi-client project (i.e. 'directed' consulting commissions to a particular group of clients whereby data are collected and experience gained) focused on several Swedish service organisations. A preliminary report on this project appeared in 1977 (Normann 1983; 1991: 11) when Normann was working as a consultant at SIAR. He worked in SIAR between 1967 and 1980, and has since 1980 run SMG (together with various associates and partners over the years).[2] This means that Normann's training as both academic and consultant, and the service multi-client project which preceded the publication of *Service Management*, took place within SIAR. The book was published three years after Normann had founded SMG, but its production process started much earlier: it can even be said to have begun before 1977 when the particular service project was initiated. In this regard Normann's life story can in various ways be said to have influenced his way of writing. However, we shall here enter the context in which Normann served his professional apprenticeship. This means that we first follow the development of SIAR from the time when Normann was employed in the mid-1960s to when he left. Then we briefly examine the development of SMG until the early 1990s in order to consider the relationhip between the text of *Service Management* and the further development of Normann's consulting business.

## Action-research

In 1966 Richard Normann had just obtained his bachelor's degree in business administration at Lund University, and began working as an assistant to Eric Rhenman (the founder of SIAR). This occasion can be seen as the starting point of the process which resulted seventeen years later in the publication of *Service Management*. Of course, Normann had earlier experiences which may have been important, but this was his first professional move and we here limit the examination of the production process to events in his professional life.

In 1967 Normann was formally employed at SIAR when their second office was established in Lund. This resulted from the appointment of Eric Rhenman as Professor of Business Administration at Lund University in 1967.[3] However, at that time he had been associated with the department for two years as reader (preceptor). Nevertheless, SIAR existed before the Lund establishment. In this regard, if we would understand what Normann joined in 1966 and what ambitions there were behind SIAR, it is important to consider how it all started.

The explicit foundation of SIAR took place in Stockholm and can be dated to 1966 when Eric Rhenman and four of his collaborators in an action-research oriented project took the group and its activities with them when they left the Stockholm School of Economics (SSE). SIAR was thereby a re-organisation of what they had already been doing for two years at SSE. Thus it seems that the context that Normann joined when he was employed at SIAR in Lund in 1967 was initiated even before the foundation of SIAR.

SIAR's pre-organisation, i.e. the action-research group at SSE, began in 1964 when Eric Rhenman took up a position at SSE Research Institute as head of a research team in administration (Gruppen för Administrativt Arbete, or GAU). The creation of GAU was an attempt to transfer to Sweden the American idea of a contract research institute.[4] The main purpose of the organisation was stated in a newspaper interview where Rhenman argued that:[5]

> There is a need to understand the actions of companies so that we can evaluate effects of different operations and there is a need to develop better instruments for managers to use.
> The research group should develop useful tools for managers who work with long-term planning, and train them if necessary.

In another interview, he stressed that clients should be enabled to influence the direction of research, thereby giving rise to important work. Rhenman also regarded this as a healthy approach to research because he believed in competition between research institutes and research companies. Furthermore, he considered this to be the most successful kind of research. Eight areas for the development of the research group were set forth:[6]

Studies of the Eskilstuna Central Hospital; Long-term planning for civil service departments; Future computer needs in local banks; Plans for the evolution of and methods of organising development programs in government business departments; Development of Pert/Cost systems for a large technological development program; Experiments in simulations of organisational planning; Development of CEO education programs; Development of forecasting methods for long-term organisational planning.

However, GAU's and Rhenman's approach proved controversial at SSE, since the policy of the school was to maintain boundaries with consultancy by requiring that the results of all research projects should be published (Söderlund 1989: 50; R3). So the group and its activities moved away from SSE, and SIAR was created in 1966 as an independent action-research institute.

In terms of methodology, the SIAR group adopted the clinical research method at an early stage. In other words, they produced case reports of organisational processes through studies of documents and interviews, and then diagnosed the organisation's 'health'. This resulted in an approach which Mintzberg (1990: 168) described as consisting of a culturally oriented conceptual framework, an open-ended style of theorising, and a methodology based on a few intensive case studies (see also Lind and Rhenman 1989).

In the early years there was a heavy emphasis on research and concentration on specific questions and areas. Throughout these years an unwritten law prevailed that all employees should write licentiate or doctoral dissertations (R12). The expectation was that all project leaders should hold either doctoral or licentiate degrees (Stymne 1995). This was also expressed by one respondent who said (R12):

> It was not directly an order [to write a thesis] but the environment was like that. Everybody had scientific ambitions, research was more significant than economic aspects. ... We were very research oriented [and] learning was in focus. Everything we did was done with a scientific approach, thus the atmosphere was some kind of a twilight zone between real academia and real practice. We were very excited when something went wrong. It was bad for the client. But we got a solid problem to solve. We had found something interesting.

Such occasions were regarded as 'opportunities to develop new knowledge since this attracted reflections and scrutiny of the ideas tried on the client' (*ibid.*). The same respondent also said that even if this approach was regarded by some clients as rather bohemian and unprofessional, it did not affect the projects since 'learning was in focus' for all activities pursued by SIAR.

Another significant manifestation of this research orientation was the habit of continuously documenting observations, meetings and consulting experiences. This habit was systematised and all memos were published in a series of internal publications, a set of working papers entitled 'Utrednings- promemoria' or UPMs (investigation memos). There was a routine whereby all UPMs, experiences and reflections from almost every commission were discussed at internal 'clinical seminars'. The ideas and experiences which emerged from these seminars were also the basis of publications by SIAR members. Stymne (1995) writes that these seminars were often attended by researchers from other disciplines and by foreign guests; sometimes even by the clients. He also writes that this was a compulsory routine that preceded all projects. Another example of the research orientation is that during this early period different methods of collecting data were tried; these also affected diagnoses of the health of clients. For instance, one project tested different interviewing techniques, then compared the results from different interviews. The main conclusion was that almost no respondents started talking until the tape recorder was switched off (R12).

The activities in the early years were financed from different sources. At the outset GAU received funding from a research council, Personaladministrativa Rådet (the Council of Personnel Administration) and Ekonomiska Forskningsinstitutet (the Economic Research Institute) at SSE. Later on, some research projects obtained grants from private scholarships, industrial organisations and research councils.[7] SIAR associates also taught at SSE and the universities of Lund and Stockholm (R4). This gave opportunities to conduct more academic-oriented research (Stymne 1995). But, even in the consultancy projects, which was yet another way to finance the institute, every chance for research was taken. This is expressed by one respondent as 'if any money was left from the consulting assignments it was used for doing research' (R12). Besides, there was an ambition to restrict external activities and SIAR staff members were paid a fixed salary, i.e. external compensation reduced their pay from the organisation (R4). An employee of long standing described the early period as follows (R9):

In the early years the direction towards development of knowledge was strong, commercialism and profitability did not guide the commissions, it rather restricted the possibility of working with interesting and thrilling questions.

Another said (R6):

SIAR was the most interesting place in the world to work in at this period ... it was a melting pot for new ideas and methodologies.

Throughout the late 1960s, SIAR maintained a practice of publishing the results of its consulting activities, and their position on the Swedish management consulting market was rather unproblematic. There was no real competition, and the kind of service they offered to their clients was unique. The profile of SIAR was at this time (1966–70) mainly academic, which means that the development of knowledge was in focus and that they had an open dialogue with the established international research community in organisation theory. Being accepted in the academic world was regarded as the quality control of SIAR's conceptual framework. Besides, the various academic activities established a knowledge base at SIAR. However, around 1970 this academic profile was sometimes considered as bohemian by its clients. In the early years this was not experienced as a problem by SIAR, but over time, clients who had already had dealings with SIAR were not as keen to engage them a second or a third time for another round of experimental searching for knowledge. After all, it was the clients who were paying for the party, and they wanted results from which they could benefit (R10/11).

The academic orientation was, however, successful insofar as a number of studies were published and circulated in Sweden as well as on the international scene. Examples in this regard are Rhenman's synthesis of SIAR's research to date (1974 [1969]) and Stymne's doctoral dissertation (1970).[8] Another example is Normann's licentiate thesis from 1969 which also yielded an article published in the *Administrative Science Quarterly* (Normann 1971). Moreover, a number of foreign scholars visited SIAR. Among them were Walter Buckley (cf. Buckley and Sandkull 1969), Alvin Zander from Ann Arbor, and Larry Bennigson, Larry Greiner and Jay Lorsch from Harvard, each of whom stayed for at least a year. Chris Argyris (Harvard) visited SIAR for shorter periods. Several of the guests

(Buckley, Bennigson and Greiner) also participated in consulting activities (R12).

Acceptance by academia was not only manifested in publications and visitors. SIAR associates were also offered academic positions. As the founding father, Eric Rhenman was first in this regard when in 1966 he became an associate professor at SSE, and at the age of thirty-three in 1967 was offered a chair at Lund university. A few years later (1974–6) he was Visiting Professor at Harvard and was also offered a full chair.[9] Nevertheless, he turned this down and concentrated instead on the growth of SIAR as a consulting organisation.

The success of *Organisation Theory for Long-range Planning* (Rhenman 1974 [1969]) can be seen as the end of an era at SIAR. At the time of its publication in the late 1960s, SIAR's financing through consultancy was more established, and Rhenman began to emphasise that the main purposes of SIAR's activities were to carry on action-research, not to produce dissertations (R9). Thus the focus of the activities shifted from 'searching for answers' (the role of the researcher) to 'giving answers' (the role of the consultant) which means that SIAR increased its work in consultancy (R9). One reason was that the great attention attracted by the work done by members of SIAR in both academia and in practice conferred legitimacy on the concepts and theories presented in the books. They felt that (R12):

What we are doing is right, and there is so much left to do.

### Business orientation and consultation

*Organisation Theory for Long-range Planning* was widely circulated, and can be considered as a synthesis of work done by SIAR members. It can also be regarded as an articulation of SIAR's body of knowledge, and thereby as the foundation upon which a more professional consulting organisation was intended to be built. One concrete manifestation of this tendency was the emergence of an explicit aim to make SIAR's consulting activities more efficient and professional. With this in mind a special company, SIAR Planning Inc., was founded in 1970 (R6). This explicit consulting organisation was owned by the SIAR foundation (60 per cent), Eric Rhenman (30 per cent) and Richard Normann (10 per cent). Thus Normann and Rhenman became the two leading figures in this new organisation. A new era had therefore begun, since the earlier principle had been that consultancy and research were treated as two important activities which in a combination comprised a successful strategy for the development of knowledge. However, around 1970 there seems to have been an increasing tendency to scrutinise rival consultancy firms (R12). Among these, American firms such as McKinsey and Co. appear to have served as the model for a high-quality consulting firm. This development is likely to have resulted from internal ambitions within SIAR for organisational growth, as well as pressure from clients that SIAR should exhibit more standard consultant behaviour.

Not all of the associates approved of the increase in SIAR's consulting orientation. One of them was Bengt Stymne, who had played a very important part in the development of SIAR's scientific profile. After defending his thesis in 1970 he was offered a position at SSE and left SIAR for a more research-oriented career (R2). Similarly, Christer Olofsson had resigned a few weeks earlier, apparently due to the diminishing degree of research orientation, but also due to the limited scope for personal development (R4). Other resignations soon followed. In 1969 and 1970, a total of thirteen people left SIAR after having worked there for an average three years, i.e. for almost two-thirds of the organisation's existence.[10] This was no doubt a considerable defection, which some of the respondents described as the 'cultural revolution' (R10–11) and others (R12) as the breakdown of a family structure where 'Rhenman was the father and Stymne the big brother, the assistants merely brothers and a few uncles were just engaged on the board'.

Those who remained tended to be more oriented towards consulting than those who had left. In addition, particularly in conjunction with some industrial studies, a number of persons who were more practically oriented were recruited in the early 1970s. The research connection was, however, also maintained through the recruitment of young Ph.D.'s or postgraduate students, primarily from Lund University (e.g. Lars Bruzelius and Per-Hugo Skärvad) but also from Stockholm University (e.g. Lars Åhrell and Sten Söderman).

While Eric Rhenman remained the undisputed leader, Richard Normann became increasingly important for SIAR's development. Previously an assistant to Rhenman, he now became a partner and chief executive officer for SIAR's consulting activities. He was in charge of the Lund office of SIAR in the early 1970s, and when greater attention was devoted to consultancy he became the first manager of SIAR Planning in 1970. In 1976 he became overall chief executive officer for SIAR.

But even though the emphasis was on consultancy, many SIAR associates were in the early 1970s still sharing their time between work at SIAR and teaching at universities. This arrangement also

implied that junior employees were still expected to write disserta-
tions based on their SIAR experience.[11] In this sense it was important
that Normann was involved in the doctoral programme at the
Department of Business Administration at Lund University as tutor.
He was also very active in discussions on methodological issues (e.g.
Normann 1970).[12]

Despite the persistent association with Lund University, the early
1970s can be said to have involved the start of a new era at SIAR,
with efforts to make consultancy more efficient and to stabilise
income. This in turn was linked to a desire for expansion (R11). In
order to improve efficiency, the establishment of work routines and
the standardisation of a set of analytical techniques were introduced
(Lind and Rhenman 1989: 171). Thus even relatively new employees
could be trusted with diagnostic work. The techniques included
analyses of company history, a product/market matrix, and cash flow
(R12, R16). Nevertheless, even though 'the cultural revolution' of
1970 initiated a change of focus of SIAR's activities towards
concentration on consultancy, the tradition of writing UPMs
continued, as well as discussions and reflections of the experiences at
the clinical seminars. This culture was so institutionalised that no
report (at least concerning larger projects) could be handed over to a
client before it had been discussed at a clinical seminar (R10). In this
respect, one respondent said that each consulting commission was also
regarded as a research project. Furthermore it should be noted that
Richard Normann's doctoral dissertation of 1975, published as a
book, *Skapande Företagsledning* (English version: *Management for Growth*
[1977]) was produced under these circumstances (R10).

### Expansion, internationalisation and standardised consultation

The period up to 1975, when Normann defended his doctoral
dissertation, was still characterised by the conceptualisation of new
ideas and the development of theories, even though the focus of SIAR's
consultancy service gradually shifted to a more orthodox consultation,
developing techniques and work routines which were more
'professional' – more set, effective and clear. But there was diminishing interest in using accumulated experience from consulting
assignments to develop new general knowledge on how organisations
work (R10/R11).

An explanation for this is provided by one respondent (R12) who
said that the clients became more demanding over time. Other reasons

mentioned were that SIAR had already been involved with many companies and that the potential clients wanted something new to prolong the commission. There was also a higher general level of knowledge inside companies in the mid-1970s than five years earlier. In addition, competition in the consultancy industry was increasing, since large American consulting firms such as Arthur Anderson, Boston Consulting Group and McKinsey operated more actively and systematically in order to earn market shares in Scandinavia. On the other hand, developments in the academic world had also been extensive in recent years – i.e. the 'competition' had increased – and the publications of members of SIAR became more independent of academia.

Consulting projects also tended to become larger in the early 1970s. A number of projects were oriented towards the restructuring of Swedish industries. One of the prestigious projects of this period was a study of the organisation of UNICEF (SIAR 1975). Indeed, this was considered a major breakthrough for SIAR (Argyris and Schön 1978). The body of knowledge developed by SIAR members at this time therefore enjoyed a good reputation in the academic world and also among those in need of highly qualified consultants.

Despite this good reputation SIAR's financial position was not stable. Income from clients did not harmonise with the practice of giving discount offers and with the expenses incurred (R6) and its financial affairs were described as more or less bohemian (R10, R11, R12). This state of affairs was unsatisfactory and Normann (at that time CEO for SIAR Planning) said that one way of stabilising finances was to organise routines and increase discipline in consultancy. SIAR Planning had been founded for this purpose in 1970, but the situation was obviously not satisfying five years later. This was one important aspect which prompted Eric Rhenman to initiate more international projects. He thereby sought to have a broader market for assignments and to be able to follow the Swedish companies in their internationalisation. As a result, offices were established in Helsinki (1970), London (1972), Copenhagen (1972), Boston (1974) and Manila (1975). The Boston office was a consequence of Rhenman's affiliation to Harvard.

It has already been mentioned that Richard Normann during this period, i.e. from 1970 onward, became a leading figure in SIAR side by side with Eric Rhenman. This was not only manifested in his position as CEO for SIAR Planning and later CEO for the mother organisation (the SIAR foundation); he also assumed a greater responsibility for passing on the tradition of synthesising consulting experiences in written form. His doctoral dissertation (Normann 1975

[1977]), a kind of sequel to Rhenman (1969b), provides the main evidence in this context.

According to two of his former colleagues at SIAR, his dissertation could be described as a synthesis of the ideology of SIAR as a consultancy firm pursuing clinical research. It thereby articulated the conceptual framework which the employees of SIAR worked within (i.e. SIAR's internal set of beliefs) – or should have – as point of departure for their consulting activities (R10–11). Interestingly enough, this work was not originally intended as a thesis, but was regarded as such by the academic community and was successfully defended in 1975. According to the author himself, he was more or less 'persuaded' to issue the thesis as a book. It has become a bestseller and in 1991 was – still in its original version – in its eighth Swedish edition, the most frequently used management book at Swedish universities during the academic year 1991–2 (cf. Chapter 4 of this volume); a ninth edition appeared in 1993. No doubt it also helped to promote a more concise SIAR identity.

If Rhenman and his publications (e.g. 1969b) was significant for the development of SIAR in the early years, Normann and his book *Management for Growth* can be said to have had a similar importance in the mid-1970s, although Rhenman was still present and chairman of the institute.[13] Thus it was not part of a 'cultural revolution' as Rhenman's book seems to have been, although it appears to have marked the end of yet another era in SIAR's history. The research orientation was thereafter further reduced, as manifested by, for example, the gradual disappearance of clinical seminars. In the words of one respondent (R11): 'the intense coaching in the ideology of SIAR lasted until Normann's dissertation in 1975 and then diminished'. An important reason for this development was probably Rhenman's decision in 1976, at the age of forty-four, to relinquish his chair at Lund, and remain associated with the department as Adjunct Professor. This was at the same time as he turned down the offer of a chair at Harvard.[14]

Now SIAR became even more oriented towards consulting: this was reinforced by an internationalisation process whereby new offices were established in Paris (1978), Milan (1979) and Singapore (1981).[15] Once again, clients' demands appear to have provided the impetus. A number of SIAR's clients expanded to other countries, and the SIAR management considered it necessary to go with them. As regards establishment in the Far East, the fact that the Swedish forestry industry had increasing interests in the area seems particularly important (R16).

These links to specific clients also prompted SIAR to build up a knowledge of conditions and developments worldwide in a number of industries. The forestry industry was not an isolated example and there were several others such as steel, shipbuilding and healthcare. This became part of a new approach, i.e. to examine strategic conditions in different industries (Lind and Rhenman 1989: 171–3). In this respect persons with experience in forestry, steel and shipbuilding were employed. The reason was that clients demanded at least as great a knowledge of a certain market or industry as they had themselves if they were to pay for consultant services (R12).

Despite the tendencies towards diversification and internationalisation in SIAR after 1975, efforts continued in research and scholarly writing. For this purpose, Rhenman gathered some Ph.D.s and a few senior consultants in 'The SIAR Think Tank Division', a part of the organisation described as a place 'where you do not earn money, but where you get famous' (R11). Another part of the organisation with a similar purpose was SIAR II or SIAR Societal Organisation, where a few other old-timers were active.

Rhenman himself appears to have taken little interest in the think tank. Instead, he worked mainly by himself on a book, with the preliminary title of *Corporate Growth Mechanisms*, which was thought to be a sequel to his 1969 book on long-range planning. However, it was never published, probably due to a fear of revealing too many of SIAR's business ideas to competitors (R11), although the ideas and concepts were used internally (R10, R11). It is also likely that the work of developing SIAR into an internationally well respected consulting firm had a negative influence on Rhenman's writings at the time.

Thus scientific production was markedly reduced in the late 1970s. At the same time, it seems clear that the competence of the organisation both with respect to methodology and in scientific terms was much greater then than in the 1960s. However, the time and interest of SIAR consultants *vis-à-vis* the academic literature seem to have drastically declined. Two factors are probably behind this development: first, tougher competition for projects, and second, rising standards in the academic world (R12). It thus seems fair to say that none of the SIAR publications after 1975 were in the forefront of research as they had been around 1970.

During the late 1970s, i.e. in 1978–9, efforts to produce manuals on how consulting in SIAR should be carried out were in focus, and this systematic project continued for three or four years (R10, R11).[16] The atmosphere, which at the outset had been characterised by attempts to develop knowledge and new ideas, thereby assumed a focus on development of standards for how to carry out efficient, successful consultancy.

The changes (the organisational growth, the internationalisation, and the standardisation of the consultancy) led to the resignations of some of the very senior people. The two old-timers who were involved in SIAR II and had both been in the organisation since 1965, left in 1977 to set up their own consulting business. Their departure was not dramatic and was regarded as a gradual process. Basically it meant that they continued SIAR II in their own organisation (R9).

### Normann leaves and establishes SMG

Since SIAR had become a fairly large organisation, formally structured with several international subsidiaries, in the late 1970s Richard Normann sought a more independent role. He had moved to France in 1977 and resigned from his CEO position at the SIAR institute in 1978 (R6). At the same time, in 1977, he also initiated a multi-client project focused on service companies. This was reported on in a first version in the same year, then revised a few years later (1983) and published under the title *Service Management*. In 1979 Normann also started a 'group within a group' called IMS (International Management group for Services). Normann and Rhenman then agreed that if they could not reach a solution which they could both accept regarding SIAR's future direction, then Normann would leave SIAR within a year.

A year later, on 1 April 1980, Normann left SIAR and started his own consulting firm SMG (Service Management Group). His departure was not as dramatic as it sounds, since he took the IMS group with him and organised it as an independent consulting firm. Besides, the activities within SMG did not really differ from those of SIAR. The principal difference was that SMG focused its work mainly on the service industry. In particular it was founded on the ideas of the early SIAR Planning and consequently SMG has since the outset had as its major purpose the supply of a high-quality consulting service (R5).

Thus SMG differed from SIAR Planning in its organisation. The group was a federation of companies which were owned locally by local partners. One important aspect was that the group consisted of international partners from France, Britain and Sweden. Instead of ownership constellation, as practised by SIAR in their international activities, the group was supposed to be held together by shared ideas.

In consequence, the development and articulation of general concepts was essential. This had been initiated in IMS, but was now even more important. The aim was that every local partner should work with the same ideas and concepts in their consultancy (R6, R7). This was supposed to be SMG's trademark. However, it was also stipulated from the beginning that the group would be dissolved whenever common ideas were no longer being shared among the associated partners (*ibid.*).

Under these circumstances, *Service Management* and the model it proposed, the service management system, became very important. The book articulated the ideas which the group should share. Even though the major multi-client project and the first report occurred under the auspices of SIAR, it was in the context of SMG that Normann completed the book. However, there were other reasons as well for the book's publication. It was important for the business, i.e. that potential clients should be in a position to know what they were getting if they hired SMG, and that the thoughts of Normann and his group should be clear (R6). In this regard one respondent said that the time was ripe to publish the book in 1983, since the labels and models developed by the group increased in popularity and were used by others (*ibid.*). The marketing of the book would thereby indicate the origin of the concepts and prompt potential clients to turn to the source for advice.

Thus, even though the consulting business was the core of SMG, it still laid claim to links with academia. The ordinary work in SMG was not research-oriented, but the group kept in touch with the universities through Normann's personal international academic contacts (R5). For instance, it established an SMG Research Advisory Board which in the mid-1980s consisted of Professors Michel Crozier (employed formally at SMG in the early 1990s), Eric Johnsen and Manfred Kets de Vries.[17] An earlier member of this council was Michel Maccoby (R6, R15). These individuals are invited to internal (or external) seminars to give lectures. SMG also appointed a scientific board called SMG Development. The intention was similar to SIAR's think tank insofar it would work as a research and development unit to keep pace with the activities of the consulting market, and to maintain and develop a high quality of ideas, new knowledge and concepts.[18] In particular the unit was intended to work as a centre for organising multi-client studies.

For some years the federation based on shared ideas seemed to be working well. But in the mid-1980s competition increased, and the service concept was 'felt to be watered down' (R7). This caused internal conflicts concerning the future development. One way to resolve this new situation was to carry out a new multi-client project. This took place in 1985 and was focused on business logic in the financial industry. The results from this project were planned to be published in a book written jointly by Normann and an SMG colleague with the preliminary title *Winning Strategies in Financial Services*.[19] According to Normann this book resembles *Service Management*, i.e. it is practically oriented, with no particular academic rhetoric. When it was finally published in 1994 its title was changed to *Designing Interactive Strategy: From Value Chain to Value Constellation* (Normann and Ramirez 1994). Even though it took a while for the book to be published, the concepts developed in the project have been used internally, and since 1985 when the multi-client study was carried out, the financial industry has represented 40–50 per cent of SMG's clients (R7). Another project related to SMG Development was what was called 'Business logic for invaders'. The project was run when Normann was Acting Professor in Business Administration at Lund University between 1984 and 1988. A few of his postgraduate students (some of them were consultants at SMG) and a colleague at SMG co-authored a book called *Invadörernas Dans* (*The Dance of the Invaders*) (Normann *et al.* 1989). According to the book's preface another multi-client study has been carried out within SMG called 'Business logic for innovators' (Normann *et al.* 1989: 9).[20] The results from this project were published in another co-authored book in 1994, *Knowledge and Value: A New Perspective on Corporate Transformation* (Wickström and Normann 1994).

However, as time passed the idea of organising a growing international organisation via federation, where all associates share the same ideas, became problematic. One respondent mentioned three major problems. One was the market situation where American consulting firms, especially McKinsey, were enjoying a remarkable success in Scandinavia (R6).[21] The second was that each local partner in each country had their own problems in their particular environments. The third was that the partners themselves pursued conflicting ambitions. For instance, partners in England and France in particular had ambitions more for academia than consultancy (R6). The situation deteriorated to the point that it was difficult to establish new common directions for the group (R6).

In 1988 the federation group was reconstituted in a group which was finally established in 1989. At that time the members amounted to 112 associates (R6). However, they also sought for strategic partnership in both Sweden and Europe. Almost at the same time

Normann was offered a seat on the board of SIFO.[22] This contact was initiated by a client of both SMG and SIFO, and as a result the two companies merged in the summer of 1990. Since the decision to merge with SIFO was not unanimous, some of the former SMG's partners left the new group.

An interesting aspect of this is that every multi-client project run in the frame of SMG (and its predecessor IMS) has resulted in a book. Another interesting point is that each of these projects and books also represents three core business areas in SMG consulting.[23] It is also interesting to note, concerning the more recent history of SMG, that a second, revised edition of *Service Management* was published in 1992, and that Normann himself has remarked that he is working on a sequel to *Management for Growth* (1975). Thus Normann is an active writer and has kept contact with academia from time to time through his writing. However, he does not work from within the scientific field, he works from the outside together with friends who have closer connections with academia. This means that it is primarily the pressure from the consulting context that rules his work and thereby the production of books such as *Service Management*.

### Early conclusions: from high concentration on research to standardised consultancy

How can the knowledge developed and carried in popular management books be understood if it is constructed in such a context as described above? The shift from research to consultation after the publication of Rhenman's book in 1969 was one thing, but there also seems to be a shift in terms of concentration. Before 1969 several specialised projects were carried out by different associates, each of which resulted in explicit academic publications. In other words, this period can be characterised by high concentration, i.e. specialisation on a few issues, problems, and methods of research pursued within the group. However, Rhenman's book was a synthesis of all the specialised projects and can thereby be defined as a step towards generalisation. This tradition was continued in Normann's book, but since it covered five more years of the group's aggregated consulting experience with various industries, it can be seen as even more general.

Another side of the heavier emphasis on business is an increased tendency towards standardisation of the methods, concepts and services supplied. This tendency was very obvious in SIAR in connection with the 'cultural revolution' of 1970. The first employee of SIAR Planning was hired to carry out standard investigations. In this regard the senior consultants handled relations with clients while the 'Indian', as the first employee called himself (R10, R11), did the 'fieldwork'. A manual, or an investigation map, had been developed, intended as a guide for the junior consultant to collecting data in the fields which Rhenman had indicated as important in his 1969 book, i.e. the market, the structure, the management system, the environment, and also the organisation's history.

Furthermore, a standardisation can also be observed in the writing. For instance, when comparing Normann's book with Rhenman's it can be observed that they discuss the same main issues, i.e. present the 'same' theory, although the former develops some thoughts further. However, the basic arguments are very similar. This is not strange, since Rhenman mentions Normann's licentiate thesis of 1969 as one of his most important references, and Normann mentions Rhenman as his single most important source of inspiration. Moreover, they worked closely together. Similarities can also be observed in the rhetoric. Thus the major body of knowledge appears to have been developed during the early years, i.e. the period before the publication of Rhenman's book. Consequently the major theoretical arguments which recur in Normann's book of 1975 but also in *Service Management* were articulated in Rhenman's book. In this regard Normann's argument can be described as a further standardisation of Rhenman's theses, i.e. the same theses are 'repeated' and 'conceptualised' to more standardised models of how organisations function and can be managed.

However, the multi-client project on service organisations which Normann initiated in 1977, and which later led to the foundation of SMG and the publication of *Service Management* in 1983, was a shift back to higher concentration; not for SIAR, but for Normann himself. For SIAR this project meant even more generalisation, since they acquired business competence in yet another area. Initially this 'group within a group' was involved in consultancy in the service industry. However, it is true that the model presented in *Service Management* is mainly concerned with discussing service organisations (i.e. a concentration on objects can be observed), but the model can be defined as general since it covers discussions and suggestions concerning how entire organisations function and can be managed. In other words, it specialised in objects (service organisations) but generalised in theories. But, along with expansion and increased competition SMG also moved towards less concentration on objects, since one of their most important arguments was that almost any organisation could be treated as a service organisation. This means that a car manufacturer, for example, not only builds cars but also produces travelling services. Yet they still have their special competence in the more traditional manufacturing industry, but with a much broader battery of standard services tuned to the results of the manufacturing. Initially they offered chiefly strategic and general advice on issues of organisational structure (R6). But after expansion, involving two other multi-client projects, joint relations with consulting firms in other disciplines and in countries where SMG do not have their own offices, and after the merger with SIFO, they are now able to offer general services in most areas where their clients need support. This means that although there was a concentration on service organisations there was a generalisation in services. However, since they suggested that almost any organisation produces a service, they did not only concentrate on the service industry.

It can therefore be argued that the context in which *Service Management* was created (SIAR and SMG) gradually developed towards lower concentration on the problems, issues, methods and objects in focus. To conclude, along with an increased business orientation, a heavier emphasis on generalisation and standardisation emerged, namely a focus on uniqueness and research attitudes relevant to more professional consulting behaviour. In this regard it seems fair to say that the situation from 1970 onwards can be described by stating that the standardisation of already achieved knowledge became more important than the development of new knowledge.

## Doing business and being modern: what makes popular management books what they are

Thus far the story has been told of how popular management books are made, while in the remainder of the chapter we shall attempt to analyse what makes them. It would appear that semi-academic contexts host or foster many of the authors whose books achieve great popularity, especially those who reach some kind of national or international guru status. As was shown in the SIAR and SMG case, the core struggle in such contexts seems to concern the relationship between making research and doing business, while the strategy to realise this scenario seems to be generalisation in topics and standardisation in concepts. In this case, it seems that first business was seen as a way to pursue research, then research (already completed) was seen as a way to pursue business. Consequently, the research institute founded in 1967 gradually tended towards consultancy (business) and away from academically oriented research. So, what makes the resultant popular books what they are? Below we will first discuss endogenous factors and then make an attempt to explain the development by exogenous factors.

## Motives, considerations and internal social forces

The search for reasons why certain moves were taken in the context discussed above yields several motives which seem to have been of particular importance. First, one of the fundamental reasons for starting an action-research institute in 1964 was articulated by the founder of SIAR, Eric Rhenman as being that he and his group had ambitions to develop 'better instruments for managers to work with, and to train them if necessary';[24] moreover, the work within the group should be performed in close collaboration with practitioners to enable them to influence the research focused on 'practical relevant questions'. Second, another important motive consisted of a strong belief, as expressed in both Rhenman (1969b; 1973a) and Normann (1975; 1977), that 'good' companies are seen as tools to improve the quality of society. This can be interpreted as meaning that both Rhenman and Normann saw themselves and their colleagues as 'messengers' of how 'good' companies should grow. In another manifestation of this motive, Normann said that he has always struggled to acquire an international reputation as an interesting person who thinks interesting thoughts on management. Similarly, Rhenman was described as aspiring to be something of a social reformer. Third, Normann gave another major reason for the efforts to write by saying that this is an important way to clarify thoughts. But he also said that books are an important marketing instrument for the consulting business. Fourth, another important motive seems to have been a continuous struggle towards organisational growth of the consulting business.

In order to realise the four major aims discussed above, three considerations of particular significance to why certain moves were made seem to have been in play. First, the pursuit of academic research was the first major move in developing credible 'knowledge' of management and organisations. In this regard the application of academic rhetoric, at least initially, was important in achieving a 'quality-check' of the body of knowledge. The continuous discussion of other research, methodologies, project design, and findings from research and consulting assignments was also a substantial element. Second, another consideration was to carry out action-research as a means of involving practitioners in the research process and enabling them to contribute to the financing. This meant that mainly qualitative case studies with normative (diagnostic) ambitions were carried out. Third, over time and along with increased business orientation, generalisations were considered regarding the problems and objects covered and the standardisation of work routines, investigation methods and models. This process was closely related to the transformation of the body of knowledge into professional codes which all employees should be able to apply, in order to offer a more professional and commercial consultancy service.

Surrounding the motives and considerations discussed above, two internal social forces can be identified. First, the personal ambitions of a few significant individuals (e.g. Rhenman and Normann) which were identified above as motives, can also be seen as social forces when they result over time in the foundation of organisations followed by their further expansion and growth. Without these forces this particular context would probably not have arisen. However, if SIAR had not come into existence something similar might have been created elsewhere by others. The reason is that this development occurred within a broader system of relations, i.e. in a larger environment, than the narrow network of links between individuals working in SIAR (and SMG), universities, business schools, friends and clients ('research objects'). In other words, the rise and organisational growth of both SIAR and SMG, and the great interest shown in books written by scholars within the SIAR-SMG context cannot be explained merely as the motives and considerations made by a few persons engendering social forces.

This leads to the discerning of a second social force, which is connected to the response provoked in both the academic and practical community by the research reports, dissertations and books written by SIAR associates. This interest appears to have engendered a feeling of legitimacy in the group. In other words, it seems that after the publication of a few licentiate (e.g. Normann 1969) and doctoral theses (e.g. Stymne 1970) and especially Rhenman's (1969b) synthesis of SIAR's aggregated knowledge, there was a feeling within SIAR that their body of knowledge was accepted as highly qualified by society at large. Normann 'maintained' this feeling through his later books, for example his dissertation (1975 [1977]) and *Service Management* (1983), which became bestsellers in the management literature genre, and are also widespread in both academia and practice. This means that the great interest attracted by these books – and thereby their considerable circulation – legitimised the body of knowledge and concepts developed in the context. This feeling seems to have been one reason for the internal ambitions of commercialisation and organisational growth which gradually led to increased standardisation of work methods and development of new 'knowledge', based on data collected by standardised methods and analysed within the framework of a standardised body of knowledge.

## Exogenous forces which prompted standardised consulting

When the competition in both academia and consultancy increased in the mid-1970s this compelled SIAR to offer more standardised and 'professional' consultancy if they wanted to remain in the consulting game as significant actors. Thus it seems fair to say that along with increased competition, i.e. when the alternatives on the market multiplied, the clients' expectations shifted as well. This can be seen as an external force, i.e. not directly caused by internal motives and considerations. However, there are other external forces for standardisation. It can be argued that the particular context studied in this chapter is a part of a larger system of relations (cf. Meyer 1994); moreover that the moves made in this context reflect in various ways what is going on in the larger system. Thus it may well be that the local context imitates patterns in the wider environment (cf. DiMaggio and Powell 1983; 1991). The course of events in the larger environment may result from general aspirations to modernity, i.e. institutionalised social patterns to search for rationality in social life (Strang and Meyer 1994).

### A struggle towards legitimacy

One obvious feature of the context discussed was that the competition increased in both fields where SIAR associates were active (i.e. the academic and the practical in combination with the popular) in the mid-1970s. At the same time there were also internal ambitions within the context of organisational growth in consultancy. Attempts to fulfil these latter ambitions had already been made, and when the competition increased in the consulting market due to the entrance of American consulting firms on the Scandinavian scene, SIAR were 'forced' by the expectations in the organisational field to take up their challenge. In other words, if SIAR wanted to remain in the game and continue growing they would have to meet the American challenge. They therefore sought to develop a more professional consulting profile, such as was characteristic of the American consulting firms. This led to the development of more standardised work routines, concepts and models, not only within SIAR but by all actors in the expanding market.

This means that a tendency of mimetic isomorphism (cf. DiMaggio and Powell 1983 [1991]) can be observed. However, to some extent we can also see this situation as coercive. What we see here is not the kind of coerciveness where there is a centre out there, such as the state, which sets rules which organisations are forced to take into account. Technically, SIAR and SMG were free to choose what to do, but in practice they had no real choice than to imitate other important actors in the field, if they wanted to compete with them. Thus it is not an external other (cf. Meyer 1996) that forces actors to do certain things in a certain way, it is the institutionalised standards in the field. Moreover, these standards tend to be ruled by the expectations of the client, that on the other hand are socially created in mental interplay with the existing supply of knowledge and the carriers of these standards and knowledge (such as the society of consultants, academics and practitioners). In other words, the increased competition obliged SIAR to standardise their work and 'imitate' the way 'professional' consultancy was performed by the Americans. It was coercive for them in the sense that if they had not made this choice, they would probably have ended up in carrying out other forms of actions and would probably not have been able to deal with the market competition.

But the American influence was not only of a coercive character. It is clear that American prototypes have been important from the beginning. For instance, the whole idea of starting SIAR was to reproduce the action-research institutes which the founder and some of his colleagues had visited in the US in the early 1960s. Similarly, another feature is that several SIAR members made study visits to American universities in the 1960s and early 1970s. Furthermore, Eric Rhenman worked as guest professor at Harvard Business School for two years in the early 1970s, while Larry Bennigson from Harvard spent a long period at SIAR in exchange. Other visitors from the US also appeared for longer or shorter periods. Moreover, the references upon which the theory and body of knowledge developed within the context were derived chiefly from books written by Americans such as Philip Selznick, Herbert Simon, James March, Richard Cyert, Chris Argyris and Donald Schön. This means that the academic interchange and the theoretical influence came mainly from the US, even though it was not the traditional mainstream (cf. Furusten and Kinch 1992) advocated by Drucker, McGregor and others. So, paths were crossed in developing the body of knowledge of which *Service Management* is a product. Mainly American paths were crossed, which is hardly astonishing since American literature, according to for example Hofstede (1980; 1990) has dominated the scene since World War II.

This development can also be explained as a process of imitation. Thus SIAR imitated action-research institutes in the US, and they imitated or at least used books by Americans as important references. In this regard, mimetic isomorphism can be observed between societies concerning the contents. Nevertheless, the American ideas were not adopted in their literal wording, i.e. they were not copied straight off. Instead it seems more fair to talk in terms of translation (Latour 1987; Czarniawska and Joerges 1996; Røvik 1998a; 1998b) when the American ideas were confronted with the consulting experiences of Swedish companies. Consequently, the activities of the Swedes were not one hundred per cent copied from the US original, but rather were edited versions (Sahlin-Andersson 1996) which had a lot in common with the original but took a slightly different form when realised in the Swedish setting.

## Being modern: towards standardisation of ideology

As already mentioned, in the opinion of one respondent (R9), after the publication of Rhenman's book in 1969 the focus of SIAR's activities shifted from 'searching for answers' (research) to 'giving answers' (consulting). Along with this shift, the culture was also described as one where the clients did not want 'more of the same' (R12). An reasonable interpretation of this seems to be that the buyers of management products do not buy 'knowledge' of how complex and difficult it is to run an organisation. They probably already know that, and instead are likely to search for sets of ideas and beliefs (ideologies) which 'give answers' to organisational problems. In this respect the development towards ideological argumentation can be explained by saying that the clients' demands are likely to be in line with the institutionalised modern ideal, where complexities in social life are 'rationally organized around notions of progress' (Strang and Meyer 1994: 107). This is often described as a consequence of modernity, i.e. the tendency to clarify the logic of situations by referring to means-ends relationships (*ibid.*: 107–8).

When observing the development of the contents of the texts created in the context (towards ideological argumentation) and the development of the atmosphere in the context (from research orientation and concentration to business orientation and standardisation) we could explain this by pointing to the tendency towards modernity in society. Thus, although this seems reasonable, its verification may need further explanations of the development of other contexts as well. However, the observation here indicates that clients search for answers which they can use to rationalise their ambiguous, and somewhat chaotic, unknown reality. In this regard, American theories inspired ideological arguments that success is related to whether management makes the 'right' or 'wrong' moves; this is what consultants seem to articulate in their writing, whether or not they are Americans themselves. Therefore, the creative process seems to be embedded in an atmosphere of offering what the clients pay for: they appear to want ideological explanations of the unknown which draw upon institutionalised myths of the omnipotent manager (myths which have originated in the US).

This tendency is hardly astonishing if we consider that the context in focus here primarily concerns commercialisation (i.e. selling) of knowledge and competence in management-related issues. In addition, managerial knowledge as a scientific field is, according to Whitley (1984a), characterised as unspecified and commonplace in comparison with, for example, physics. Therefore it is only to be expected that practitioners who live in a world of increasing complexity turn to ideologies in their search for ideas on how to solve problems. In other words, ideologies can often be seen as 'nicer' than knowledge since ideological argument circles around how things should be instead of how they are under certain circumstances. American ideologies are even 'nicer', since they ride on the air of the American dream, where everything is possible for anyone as long as they try hard and make the right moves. Furthermore, the American dream is probably more appealing than its Swedish equivalent, the Swedish melancholy and 'Jante-lagen' (a cultural 'law' that insists you should not think that you are better than anyone else).

Due to the short geographical, and often also cultural, distance between Sweden and Germany, and due to the success of the German economy, it is worth noting that no ideas from Germany have been introduced into the Swedish managerial discourse. But perhaps the view of Germans as boring technocrats is less appealing than the American dream (there could also be language barriers and historical, war-related reasons).

## Concluding remarks

The motives, considerations, social forces and institutional mechanisms in the making of books like *Service Management* shed more light on what these kinds of book represent as elements of the organisational environment. As shown in the case in focus here, they can be defined as a result of an ambition to produce practical useful instruments for organisational change. By the same token they are products of an author's ambition to earn a reputation. They can also be said to have attracted great interest (especially Normann's books). This has probably constituted a self-generating force for further struggle in the same direction. Thus success seems to have encouraged internal ambitions in business and growth. However, the increased competition in consulting and academia also appears to have been crucial, since firms wishing to remain and to grow in the consulting game were forced to put more effort into developing their consulting profile in order to become more professional. Otherwise there was a risk that clients would take their business elsewhere. This observation supports what DiMaggio and Powell (1983 [1991]) and Scott and Meyer (1983 [1991]) say concerning clients' expectations as a pressure for isomorphism among organisations in any one organisational field. Thus these expectations may be a force for standardisation of activities pursued within the field. Moreover, the tendency towards ideology and standardisation also seems to result from a broader trend in society that is often called modernity (cf. Strang and Meyer 1994), where there is a continuous institutionalised search for means-ends relationships. These do not have to be 'right' as long as they are regarded as legitimate in a social context (this will be further discussed in the next chapter).

It is perhaps only to be expected that organisational growth in consulting also involves a focus on business, which is not highly research-orientated. It may not even be surprising that in a context where the major struggle is to make business out of management 'knowledge' there is a tendency to move towards generalism and standardisation, since there are reasons to believe that consulting firms with aspirations to expand are likely to have 'professional' competence in several areas. However, it is more remarkable that the 'knowledge' produced in a context like that studied in this chapter is diffused to a vast number of people. Thus within the context there have been tendencies towards standardisation of working methods, concepts and models, which are packaged into consulting commissions, advice, and texts which reach many people in various positions and situations in society. How can this be explained? Why do popular books take similar forms?

One important influence in the development of the context was client expectation. In combination with increased competition in the marketplace, internal ambitions of organisational growth, and the authors' personal ambitions to acquire a reputation, it seems to offer answers, i.e. ideological arguments for how things are, in a standard-ised way (i.e. what other 'professional' consultants do, and what the clients expect of a 'professional' consultant) and depict what is likely to emerge from such a process.

# 7 What do popular management books mean for organisations?

## Introduction

The chief aim of this study purports, through the search for characteristics of the supply of popular management books, to discern what these mean for organisations. This is discussed throughout the study in terms of the model introduced in Chapter 1 (Figure 1.1) and scrutinised in Chapters 2 and 3. In this model, the general managerial discourse was seen as the accumulation of textualisations of managerial and organisational life, and as such, being an element of the institutional environments of organisations. Moreover, in this regard it was seen as the framework within which the production, diffusion and consumption of managerial manifestations takes place. As a reminder of the limitations of this study, we here focus on managerial manifestations as such (popular books in particular), not on their application by organisations. However, the consumption of popular managerial manifestations by organisations is an important component of the model if we would understand the production and diffusion processes. Thus the consumption process has not been observed empirically in this study, but will be discussed in this closing chapter, and be based on the results of the analyses of diffusion and production processes.

In this chapter we shall discuss what popular management books may mean for organisations. In this regard we concentrate on the core of the model, i.e. the interaction between the production and the diffusion of popular managerial manifestations, since this is the arena in which the empirical observations have been made. However, it has already been concluded that consumption is an important aspect of the other two processes, and thereby also becomes crucial to the discussion. But first we shall particularise the conclusions drawn in earlier chapters concerning the production and supply of popular management books. Next, starting from these conclusions, we shall explicitly discuss the relationship between the popular managerial discourse and the consumption of popular managerial manifestations by organisations. Then we shall make some observations concerning the managerial discourse, and close by suggesting that this study is not the end and that there is more to do in the field.

## Towards standardisation of production and supply

In earlier chapters of this book it has been pointed out that the general managerial discourse in Sweden is likely to be dominated by prominent voices in its popular layer. A substantial share of books stored in libraries originate from the UK but almost no other nationalities appear. When practically oriented distribution channels were observed, the Americans held pride of place, with the locals, i.e. the Swedes, close behind, no other nationalities being represented (bar one Norwegian). These results indicate that the popular managerial discourse can be characterised by a tendency towards standardisation, i.e. that popular books are either of national (Swedish in this case) or North American origin. 'Americanism' (i.e. managerial manifestations of North American origin) seems therefore to be an important dimension of the general managerial discourse. If the results from the Swedish case have wider bearing, this study illustrates a possible trend in the international managerial discourse. There are good reasons to believe that similar patterns appear in other national or cultural arenas besides that of Sweden (cf. Huczynski 1993; Chanlat 1994).

One conclusion drawn from our analysis of two popular management books representing the twin poles of 'Americanism' and 'nationalism' was that they displayed remarkable similarities. For instance, it was argued that the authors' backgrounds were very similar, and that the contents of both books could be characterised as ideological, since the authors frequently used personal experiences as empirical data and supported their arguments with metaphors, platitudes, myths, and conventional wisdom. Even though other studies may be frequently quoted, they are mainly used as arguments to support their conclusions. This means that no new ground is broken; instead the authors are likely to travel mainstream on paths well beaten by others. The similarities between the Swedish and the American book can be attributed to another standardised element of the western managerial discourse, namely a North American inspired set of ideas that says the destiny of organisations is primarily a function of the activities of their managers. However, although a great many books have been analysed, the present study only reports on two of them, and this conclusion must be seen as an indication of a trend rather than a proof thereof. Moreover, the books analysed here are a drop in the ocean compared with the total supply of books over time.

Finally we studied the context from which the Swedish book (*Service Management*) emerged. The most obvious characteristic was that the book was created within an atmosphere of increasing business orientation. For instance, one of its author's ambitions was to market his new consulting firm. However, the publication and the process behind *Service Management* was not unique in the context. It was one of a series of books produced for a similar purpose, even though its precursors had a more academic profile. Another characteristic was that the methods and work routines of the context tended to become more standardised over time. Only one context for the production of popular management books was observed in this study. But there are grounds for believing that business orientation and standardisation of methods and work routines characterise the context of production of many popular management books, since several others were produced in the same context and under similar circumstances. This is also supported by the observations in Chapter 4, which looks at a bestseller list of the top eight books published in Sweden during the 1980s (cf. Table 4.5). Three of these eight books were written by famous managers while the other five were by consultants.[1] One example is the American book (*In Search of Excellence*) which, like *Service Management*, was written with the aim of strengthening a firm's (McKinsey and Co.) position in the consultancy market. Moreover, at the same time as Peters and Waterman were writing their book, several others which also became bestsellers were produced within the same context. The most successful of these is probably *Corporate Culture* (Deal and Kennedy 1982). This suggests that there are often connections between consulting firms and bestsellers.

## Allies in the popular managerial discourse

Throughout this study it has been argued that processes of production and diffusion of managerial manifestations do not occur in isolation. Moreover, we have also mentioned that these two processes can hardly be understood unless processes of consumption are also considered. Consequently, none of these processes starts from a *tabula rasa*: producers build their arguments on already existing ideas, distributors decide what to supply from previous experience of what usually sells well, and consumers demand manifestations according to what they judge to be interesting or relevant. This means that 'new' production, distribution, and consumption processes appear within the frame of a discourse already in progress. Consequently, if we want to understand what popular management books mean for organisations, we need to discuss the interaction of these three processes.

Above it was suggested that there is a tendency to standardisation in the layer of the general managerial discourse here called the popular managerial discourse. Not only does this imply that its producers imitate each other, it also means that many people like to consume what (a few) others produce and their intermediaries distribute. In this regard it might be appropriate to compare popular managerial manifestations with more ordinary products on a market: they are demanded, produced, distributed, bought and sold. But this does not fully explain what popular management books mean for organisations. Put in other words, popular books are not only products, they also represent something the buyer either needs, believes in, cannot resist or can consume as a fashion. Moreover, a managerial manifestation cannot be consumed without being interpreted, edited and translated. However, this is a perspective on management knowledge not all are likely to agree on. There are many who believe that knowledge can be packaged in forms that can then be carried from place to place without losing their relevance and meaning, and can then be unpacked and utilised with the same results as in the original context. This is, for instance, the rationale behind a lot of management education and management consulting in the western world.

In Chapter 3, when we discussed the complexity of moving managerial knowledge in time and space, we referred to Latour and his discussion of a similar phenomenon in technoscience which can be called the black box syndrome (Latour 1987: 133). His point is that there are in society established forms of conversation – discourses – for particular objects, ideas, models or phenomena, in which 'allies' can be encountered. Allies take these forms of conversation for granted, i.e. they accept the argument and thereby close the debate into black boxes where the core arguments are not questioned. If people wish to open the boxes, to renegotiate the facts, to appropriate them, masses of allies arrayed in tiers will come to the rescue of the claims and force the dissenters into assent: but the allies will not even think of disputing the claims, since this would be against their own interests, which the new objects of knowledge have so neatly translated. Dissent has been made unthinkable. At this point, these people do nothing more to the objects but pass them along, reproduce them, buy them, believe them. The result of such smooth borrowing is that there are simply more copies of the same object.

This may explain why, as soon as anyone questions the black box, an array of the already-converted – the allies – comes forward to defend its claims. Thus the 'facts' are claimed to be 'objective truths', which means that they are not subject to interpretation within the society of allies. The black box thus constitutes a framework for the kind of knowledge that is permitted to be diffused. The logic of modernity is used in order to explain relations between means and ends. The allies accept these explanations and take them for granted. In this way certain arguments have turned into 'facts'. Latour maintains that the allies defend the 'facts', since challenging them would be against their own interest. Sometimes it may happen that they have built up their whole existence based on these facts. To open up the black boxes and reinterpret the arguments and the underlying beliefs is not in their interests. Thus the black boxes, i.e. the taken-for-granted sets of facts, are passed along, reproduced, bought and believed, and there will be many out there prepared to defend certain arguments and models. Consequently, it may be difficult to contend in an arena dominated by a powerful core of allies with a different message and rhetoric. An example in this regard could be the upstream academic, who is likely to have problems first in reaching mainstream consultants with her message, and then in getting through to practitioners who believe whatever they hear, provided it corresponds to what they already know.

Latour's scenario seems to describe very well the situation in the popular managerial discourse where tendencies to standardise can be explained by saying that a powerful core of 'allies' is in operation. This core consists of those who produce, distribute and actively consume managerial manifestations that become popular, i.e. participants in the popular managerial discourse. This core of 'allies' could also be said to consist of all those involved in the commercialisation of managerial manifestations. This means that arguments which do not support commercialisation contravene this core group's interest. In this regard, since we have observed standardisation in the discourse, we can say that by their mutual imitation the allies are repeating and thereby defending a core of arguments. Thus they 'guard' and maintain their position and established form of conversation, by reproducing, passing along, buying and believing in the institutionalised informal standards of the popular discourse.

The allies, when it concerns popular management books, are first of all the authors thereof. This study shows that management consultants constitute the major group of authors and that writing books is important for their consulting business. Indeed, they make their living by selling investigations, advice, speeches, seminars and books. This leads to another important group of allies, namely those who buy the consultants' services and books. Another group of allies comprises the publishers and distributors of management books. Yet another consists of business magazines which both report on new books and, according to Furusten and Kinch (1996) also tend to mediate information which corresponds to that which is offered in popular books. It is also worthy of note that these magazines often carry advertisements by management consulting firms, i.e. they can be seen as a marketing forum for management consultancy. This indicates that business journalists also tend to perform as allies. To summarise, there seem to be at least four groups of allies, all of which have commercial interests in the maintenance and guarding of the popular managerial discourse, i.e. the producers, the distributors, the buyers and the commentators (management and business journalists) of popular managerial manifestations.

Following Willmott (1993) who argues that paradigms in society are established through social and intellectual struggle within a wider structure of relations, it seems reasonable to infer that the groups of 'allies' just mentioned compose such a 'structure of relations' where they pass on, reproduce and buy manifestations which are in line with the established paradigm in which they move and with the discourse they transmit. A consequence of this phenomenon, whether or not the findings in this study are representative of dominant voices in the general managerial discourse, is that it is difficult to reach a wider audience for voices which advocate other messages and which traffic in a discourse and paradigm other than what is generally taken for granted and defended by these allies. In other words manifestations which do not conform to the institutionalised discourse are unlikely to reach a wide group of people (cf. Hasselbladh 1995). If this is true, since it has been concluded that ideological argument tends to predominate and is constantly maintained and guarded by the allies, it is very hard for other kinds of manifestation to be accepted as arguments of any importance by participants in this discourse. In particular this means that it is difficult to distribute knowledge, i.e. arguments characterised by cognitive rhetoric, on the popular scene, since the allies seem to prefer ideology.[2]

## Standardisation and the development of management knowledge

As argued above, the allies of popular managerial manifestations can be seen as defensive when they buy, produce, and distribute them. It could be said that they are building barriers against contradictory perspectives. Consequently, there are certain requirements an actor needs to fulfil in order to be accepted on this scene: acceptance will depend on whether the jargon of the popular discourse is accepted, i.e. that the barriers are not questioned. This means that the already existing discourse constitutes the standard for how popular textualisations of organisational and managerial life should present themselves if, for example, an author wants to see her book widely diffused. Moreover, since books which become popular tend to be created in business-oriented contexts where consultancy is the method of collecting data, this means that the clients, i.e. the buyers, will finance the production process. However, as well as authors, buyers too wish to profit from their investments. Often this means that they want some kind of advice or help in seeing their situation from another angle. Consequently, if one consultant does not give the clients what they expect, another will probably be offered the job instead. Such tendencies were observed in the analysis of the context in which *Service Management* was created. The competition in the consultancy market more or less forced the consulting firm to become more like its rivals, i.e. to develop more standardised work routines, models and analyses, since these were what the clients preferred to pay for. This was at least what the leading actors feared.

There are, of course, economies of scale for the consulting firm developing or adopting standardised routines, since inexperienced or unskilled assistants can be employed to conduct investigations by following standard manuals. However, there is also a risk in creating managerial manifestations in this way, since the information sought may also be that found (cf. McCloskey 1986). This means that the employment of standardised work routines and manuals will yield standardised data. Consequently, standardised data may be collected and compared with a standardised and taken-for-granted model of how things should be. In other words, the judgements of consultants concerning whether or not an organisation is healthy depend on how the organisation relates to the standard requisites for good and bad management. Such an approach is risky, since the standardised data collected may not be the most relevant to every organisation. Moreover, the standardised model may not illustrate the positive or negative aspects of all organisations. The reason is that circumstances not included in the standardised methodology and analytical model are not considered, even though these neglected aspects might very well be important for the forces involved in an organisation's development. However, even though the tendencies of standardisation may be risky, this may well be the only way for a consulting firm to stay in business, since this is what the clients are likely to pay for. As shown by the case study, the assumption that the consulting firm possesses a unique body of knowledge is common. It seems to fit well with institutionalised standards in the international popular managerial discourse. This implies that in terms of content a client is likely to get the same wherever he or she turns. There might still, however, be important differences between the performance of consultants; and how they perform probably does influence the way clients edit and translate the standardised knowledge they carry. Thus in-firm standards are likely to correspond to institutionalised professionalism in international management consulting. Although this does not make the body of knowledge in each firm unique, it may still appear new and unknown to the client, since the value of the contents can only be judged by its social relativity in each situation.

Even though the value of a certain managerial manifestation is local, it is still of importance to examine the discourse at the general level. If manifestations are based on data collected in this way it is fair to say that there is a risk that the development is founded on idealised data, i.e. on data which conform to the standardised model. In other words it seems that paths trodden by scholars who stress contradictory arguments are avoided (not crossed), at least in overt references in the texts. This observation supports Kennedy's (1991: xiv) observation in her study of management gurus, namely that the gurus mainly base their arguments on each other's and their own. In other words paths not supporting the mainstream of the predominant general discourse are avoided. Latour (1987) attributes this to the fact that it is not in their interest to position their arguments to contradictory references since their own credibility could thereby be questioned, which in this case would adversely affect their consulting business.

To conclude, data collected by standardised methods and models, which are compared with standardised models of how things should be, could imply that the notion of an ideal organisation (i.e. the discourse's standard for what is taken for granted as good and bad) is reproduced, passed on and thereby preserved in the production of new manifestations. This may explain why voices that become popular are transmitted in general and ideological arguments, since general arguments can hardly be denied, especially not in a commonplace field like management studies (e.g. Whitley 1984a; 1984b). In other words general standards may well be the best managerial goods to sell since it is easier to defend general than specific arguments. However, it also seems fair to say that this tendency can probably be observed in other situations as well. For instance, it happens that more research-oriented scholars pursue similar lines, i.e. they take a mainstream course in their respective fields, in both the general discourse and in narrow, specialised discourses (particular discourses related to a certain topic or research problem). Nevertheless, the case analysed in this study is believed to be representative of the production of popular managerial manifestations in modern society; but, again, to confirm the general tendencies indicated here it would probably be useful to make comparative studies with other contexts.

Following from the discussion in this section, a complexity for the development and prevalence of management knowledge can be particularised, i.e. if people prefer ideological arguments on general issues, will this encourage scholars and others working with textualisations of organisational and managerial life to search for explanations beyond the popular managerial discourse? Should we be satisfied with repeating and passing on the obvious – what is institutionalised as conventional wisdom – or should we try to understand organisational development in the abstract? It is hard to judge what is right and wrong here, but it is important to not take the message proposed by these allies for granted, especially since the basic assumptions in the standardised model have been questioned in many studies carried out over the last three decades. There are better, or at least other explanations than the standard. In many situations it might be more relevant to not just skim the waves, but to delve further and see what lies beneath. However, in other situations what is most important may be to follow the standard, even though there are more relevant models known and available. This paradox will be further elaborated below. But first we will discuss more in detail what triggers the tendencies towards standardisation in the processes of production and diffusion.

## Consumption prompts standardisation

Hitherto the complexity of the consumption of managerial manifestations has only been mentioned in passing since the empirical focus has been on characteristics of their supply and production. However, as will be emphasised in what follows, consumption is a part of the other two processes and cannot be isolated from them. In other words these processes are symbiotic, even though the analyses here imply that consumption guides the development of production and supply. This is contradictory to the ideal view, where knowledge is first created scientifically and then diffused to other scholars, or even to the general public in popular and more accessible forms (cf. Whitley 1985). Thus the ideal view is that consumption of knowledge is the final process, i.e. production, diffusion, and consumption take place in isolation and are joined to each other as three separate links in a chain. This would also mean that popular manifestations represent knowledge, albeit in a popularised form. However, the observations of the present study reveal another pattern. We have argued that these groups of allies consume what other voices in the popular discourse have already produced. What they consume, however, is not just anything. In fact, they tend to consume manifestations that have gained informal acceptance as representing a general knowledge. Manifestations that have achieved high circulation in the form of books, or that are written by famous managers or well known management gurus, are most likely to achieve such a status.

But producers of managerial manifestations, such as the authors of books, are not the only category of consumer. Another important category is represented by practitioners in organisations, from chief executives, personal managers and managers-to-be, to others who have a particular interest in management issues. This is probably the largest group of consumers; and they buy the manifestations in large quantities, thus financing both the processes of distribution and production thereof.

In Chapter 6 it was shown that consumer demand dictates what will be diffused and created, and it has been noted that ideological explanations are preferred to cognitive ones. Allies with a commercial interest in defending dominant ideological standards appear in all three processes of production, distribution and consumption. In this way they contribute to the maintenance and guarding of these standards. Consequently, it can be argued that the popular discourse impedes the prevalence of knowledge in modern society, since there is a large core of allies (the creators, distributors, consumers and commentators) who tend to reject any argument that contradicts their commercial interest and paradigmatic belonging. Since it is the consumers who finance the other processes, this means that they have considerable impact on what the others do. This pact between consumers, producers, distributors and commentators thereby works as something of a fire door that keeps new knowledge or contradictory arguments at bay. In this way it also becomes an obstacle to the creation of knowledge since it promotes standardised frames of reference, standardised forms of conversation, and standardised work methods and routines. The buyers, i.e. the final users, are the most powerful category of actors in this system, since they talk in terms of money and are thereby able to dominate the agenda in the discourse and judge its quality. The popular discourse thus becomes somewhat esoteric since the same arguments are shuffled around and repeated continuously, which makes it difficult to function on this scene by stressing contradictory perspectives, i.e. non-ideological viewpoints.

## Organisations and standardised discourse

With the discussions above in mind we may now attempt to particularise what popular management books — and thereby popular managerial manifestations and the popular managerial discourse — tend to represent as elements of the organisational environment.

If the above conclusions hold true for a wider population of voices, it is appropriate to characterise the popular managerial discourse as mainly a route for distribution of standardised ideological representations of managerial life. This means that, due to their wide diffusion, they probably dominate the general discourse in which norms for good and bad organisation and management are articulated. Furthermore, since similarities occur among these articulations, it seems reasonable to argue that popular voices on managerial and organisational life in modern society can be regarded as important policy makers (DiMaggio and Powell 1983 [1991]), fact builders (Latour 1987) or opinion leaders who create and maintain cultural expectations, norms and standards of good and bad management and organisation. In this way it can be argued that prevalent voices in the popular discourse are important contributors to the structuring of cultural elements in organisations' institutional environments. Thus it can be argued that this structuring originates in, refers to and re-articulates North American managerialism.

What does this mean for organisations? One possibility is that North American managerialism may be a point of departure for people's expectations of what managers should do and how leadership should be conducted. In this respect it may be so that managers, in order to acquire legitimacy, must meet these expectations in one way or another. Most of these expectations are probably taken for granted and therefore routine, and may occur in the practical and popular discourse almost as if they were natural objects. This means that some expectations might be very obvious and thereby powerful in regard to what managers must do to acquire legitimacy in particular situations;

in other words they have become institutions. For instance, one such widely institutionalised notion is that a manager is supposed to be more or less omnipotent: the prevailing view of the manager in the general discourse presents him as a powerful 'tamer' who has the ability to 'read' reality, and from this create the 'right' organisational values, structures and actions and thereby steer the firm towards success. In this regard there seems to be a uniformity in the voices which predominate in the general managerial discourse. Although no organisation is obliged to meet these expectations, they may have little choice, since managers who do not take this route could have difficulty acquiring legitimacy (cf. Meyer and Rowan 1977 [1991]).

Further, tendencies to standardisation may be of considerable importance in processes of uncertainty-avoidance. When difficulties arise in an organisation and the atmosphere is characterised by a high degree of uncertainty, it is not unlikely that someone will search for knowledge of how to solve the problems. In such situations this person (or group of persons) will probably turn for advice to prominent voices in the popular discourse. They might hire consultants, attend or send staff to external management development programmes, or buy literature and business journals. If the popular managerial discourse tends to be standardised – as indicated in this study – then those persons who turn to voices therein for advice are likely to encounter uniform suggestions, which will reduce uncertainty. In other words, if the answers received correspond to commonsense and institutionalised expectations, and are uniform, they will be considered to represent a correct view of how management and leadership works. In this regard it is possible that such manifestations, held by many individuals and organisations, will be believed worthy of imitation. It may feel comfortable and encouraging to try to solve problems in a way which is held to be correct by the general discourse, since many other organisations have done likewise. Consequently – if many individuals and organisations imitate the same norms, role-models, ideologies and conceptual framework – there may also be grounds for believing that a large number of organisations are likely to develop uniform local standards concerning organisational identity, structure and activities (Meyer 1994).

However, following DiMaggio and Powell (1983 [1991]), it is also reasonable to argue that standardisation in the popular managerial discourse exerts normative isomorphic power on local organisations. In other words, due to great diffusion and uniform articulations of what management, or leadership, is supposed to be and how it should work, norms of 'good' and 'bad' are created and maintained. When people in their daily activities pass judgement on events, it might happen that consciously or unconsciously (i.e. when these norms have been institutionalised) they find arguments and motives to assess something as 'good' and something else as 'bad', and then make different kinds of moves.

To conclude, it seems that the standardised popular managerial discourse propagates institutionalised myths, beliefs, institutions and ideologies about management in the modern western world. In this respect it can be regarded as contributing to the development, maintenance and preservation of general institutions of management. These institutions are important elements in the institutional environments of organisations inasmuch as they strongly influence the norms of managerial and organisational behaviour which individuals and organisations judge as 'good' or 'bad'. Although a vast number of individuals and organisations are exposed to many voices, which pass on the predominant ideas of the standardised popular managerial discourse, this does not mean that the ideas are literally transmitted.

The discussion here has been concentrated on how the tendency to uniformity in the general managerial discourse might stimulate normative institutional mechanisms which influence organisations' situations. In consequence, standardisation in the popular managerial discourse may well also promote standardised behaviour in local organisational processes. However, even though these explanations seem reasonable, they pertain to a general level. In other words, the analysis above does not involve the complexities associated with individual interpretation and translation of observations. Instead it implies that tendencies to homogeneity on a general, macro level in society also constitute a force for isomorphism among organisations at the local level. However, as will be argued in the next section, general tendencies will not automatically spread to local processes. When individuals and organisations consume popular managerial manifestations they are likely to, as discussed thoroughly in Chapter 3, translate their meaning to suit their purposes in particular situations.

## The consumption of management standards

It has been argued above that popular managerial manifestations maintain and guard institutionalised standards in the popular managerial discourse. Thereby they can be seen as components of everyday life in many organisations. Thus the consumption of management books goes beyond those who actively buy and read them. In fact, even though it may happen that those who buy management books do not actually read them, they are still likely to consume the ideas therein, since these correspond to conventional wisdom about management and organisations. We shall in this section consider the relationship between standards in the popular managerial discourse and the consumption of these standards by organisations. In this regard the popular managerial discourse, and thereby popular managerial manifestations, are seen as both carriers and guardians of these standards and as elements in the construction of organisations. So far so good! However, as argued in Chapter 3, the existence of homogeneous ideas, such as standards, is not the same as homogeneity of actions. The nature of a standard is that it is well known and considered in different organisational settings. This means that they are likely to be components in several local and collective processes where organisations are constructed. Due to the nature of management knowledge and its capacity to be transmitted in time and space and be represented in standardised manifestations, the use of these standards in different organisations may result in different local organisational versions. According to Czarniawska-Joerges (1992a) such representations of reality are constantly subjected to interpretation by individuals who experience them in different ways. Giddens (1979: 40–1) strikes a similar note, saying that there is not one reading of a text, 'there are only readings', i.e. different interpretations of the meaning of a text. So, the adoption of a management standard is not bound to result in a standardisation of organisational behaviour (Furusten and Tamm Hallström 1996). This is somewhat contradictory to what is suggested by, for example, DiMaggio and Powell (1983 [1991]) in their discussion of mimetic and normative isomorphic pressure.

This means that it is probably not the literal wording of the standard which is applied in practice. Consequently, it matters little how 'right' a specific manifestation is, since a 'wrong' argument may cause the 'right' action (cf. Czarniawska-Joerges 1988). In this regard it could be argued that it does not matter if the ideas are based on an American setting as long as they are translated into situation-specific actions. Thus North American managerialism could still be relevant to, for example, Swedish organisations even though it does not really represent Swedish conditions. The reason is that even though an idea is 'wrong' it may be seen as more appealing than a vague 'right' explanation of reality. In this respect the 'wrong' argumentation may impel organisations to initiate certain internal processes. Such action can take various forms, ranging from individual thinking, individual and collective use of concepts or models borrowed from, say, a text on interactions between relatives, friends, colleagues or business partners, to the more or less literal application of organisational models. It can be argued that ideas are re-negotiated and edited when they are transformed from being general cultural elements in the institutional organisational environment to elements in local interaction between individuals on organisation-specific expectations of reality. In local organisational settings these expectations could concern the creation of individual and collective norms for 'good' management, 'right' leadership style, 'the best' organisation structure, 'the right' organisational goals and visions and 'the right' organisational history. Thus whether or not they end up in true accounts is not the case here!

To conclude, management standards are not likely to be consumed in organisations in their literal wording. Below, three possible relations between standards in the popular managerial discourse and local organisational processes will be discussed, namely standards and the development of local discourses, standards as symbols for meaning, and standards and the construction of organisations.

## Standards and the development of local organisational discourses

If standards are not applied in their literal wording, how then are they related to organisational processes? One possibility is that standards in the popular discourse are reflected in local organisational conversations on management. This means that individuals may mould their language on the general discourse when they interact with others. In this way individuals might 'borrow' or adopt a general language. Thus, when individuals negotiate and interact in matters of management and leadership, they may use a terminology which corresponds to the general discourse (cf. Kinch *et al.* 1998). In this way the popular managerial discourse can be seen as incorporated in processes of local social construction of reality.

If this holds true, the popular discourse can also be seen as providing the vocabulary for 'normal conversation' on organisational management. However, it is also a source of textualised ideas and concepts which individuals use and quote in processes of local interactions. In this regard it can be argued that the popular discourse constitutes a structure within which specific organisational talk is moulded. This means that the uniformity in the general discourse concerning management and leadership matters can be perceived in local conversations through individual translation. Thus it seems reasonable to allege that the language used in local settings, in negotiations on conceptual frameworks for the particular organisation and its environment, norms, goals, visions and ethics, is likely to be based on what is articulated by prominent voices in the popular managerial discourse.

This section has described the grounds for believing that the general managerial discourse is reflected in local communication within organisations. Consequently, it may be appropriate to regard them as a language or dress code, so to speak, which authorises the wearer to participate in important conversations, i.e. it is similar to wearing proper clothes, behaving properly, listening to the 'right' music, visiting the 'right' restaurants, etc. In other words it may be that popular managerial manifestations are consumed for the same reasons that trends and fashions in other connections are consumed (cf. Abrahamson 1996; Røvik 1996; Kieser 1997). However, foreign ideas take time to 'travel into an organization and become embedded in structures and activities' (Røvik 1998b: 6). This suggests that these fads may also penetrate further into the organisation and affect other activities beyond mere talk, even though they are not installed literally. We can say that the idea works like a virus with a long incubation period before its effects are made manifest. Moreover, its effects can be different depending on the condition of the host. The virus analogy suggests that an organisation passively receives a disease that infects its activities almost by nature. However, the movement of ideas into organisations can also be understood as an active process. This has been discussed in a number of studies in terms of translation (Latour 1987; Czarniawska and Joerges 1996; Røvik 1998a; 1998b) or editing (Sahlin-Andersson 1996). Ther consequences of this for local organisations are, however, likely to differ between organisations. To translate standards into a local language is one thing. To make further translations of these translations into actions is another.

### Standards as symbols of meaning

The uniformity and the ideological characteristics of arguments presented by prominent voices in the general managerial discourse may influence actions in other ways as well. Brunsson (1989), for instance, argues that talking of an event does not necessarily mean that it has happened, or that it will happen. The talk is connected to a situation, but this may be a different story to what actually has happened or will happen. Although there may be different versions of the situation in its past, its present and its future, the processes of talk, decision and action can occur in parallel since they allude to different claims from the environment. Brunsson explains that it is not always necessary for an organisation through physical actions to meet all the expectations of individuals and organisations concerning its behaviour. Sometimes these expectations are likely to be satisfied if they are merely articulated. Individuals involved in the process may thus be satisfied mentally, at least for a while.

However, it is probably not particularly convincing merely to talk in general, or any terms at all about an event. The speaker is more likely to earn credibility if he or she talks in terms of the dominating discourse (cf. Bloomfield and Best 1992). In this respect, if a manager or a consultant explains complex and ambiguous organisational events by using an institutionalised jargon in the general discourse, then the members of an organisation may accept this as credible. Consequently, if the language used by the speaker complies with generally institutionalised norms it is likely to be given legitimacy. This means that the official picture, i.e. the talk, of what the organisation is doing may touch upon norms which are imposed by participants in the organisational field. Brunsson (1989) even claims that talk can sometimes replace or support actions, by verbally, and thus also mentally, accomplishing norms which are not accomplished physically. In this respect, any current practical process which does not really correspond to institutionalised practice could be defended by talking of it in terms of this practice. So, reference to a situation as if it were something other than it really is, may make it easier to continue with the daily routine.

This is discussed further by Czarniawska-Joerges (1988; 1993). She writes that talk promotes the creation of meaning in the activities of organisations. Her point is that talk is a social action which ties the articulated activity to the physical and gives it meaning. In a similar way Pondy (1978), Pfeffer, (1981) and Smircich and Morgan (1982) argue that managers create meaning by using language and symbolic actions. This argument also corresponds to Berger and Luckmann's (1967) statement that the language is a secondary socialising activity, i.e. the meaning of reality is socially constructed through verbal interaction between people.

Thus, when standards in the popular discourse are reflected in local communication within organisations, these are then likely to impinge on the local development of language codes. These in turn are used in organisational processes in order to interpret and discuss the local business. In fact, as argued by Weick (1979b: 42):

there are distinct ways to talk about organisations. For example, an organisation can be viewed as a body of jargon available for attachment to experience.

This means that if a phenomenon is articulated by means of a particular body of jargon, it may be easier for participants to believe what they see. In this respect it is also possible to talk about corporate images in a certain organisation. Weick goes on to say that 'Managerial work can be viewed as managing myths, images, symbols and labels', and that

> the manager who controls labels that are meaningful to organiza-
> tional members can segment and point to portions of their experi-
> ence and label it in consequential ways so that employees take that
> segment more seriously and deal with it in a more organization-
> ally appropriate manner (Pettigrew 1975). Because managers
> traffic so often in images, the appropriate role for the manager
> may be evangelist rather than accountant.
>
> (*ibid.*)

The quotation implies that managers may be able to make sense of organisational activities if they can express themselves with labels which make sense to those involved (cf. Pondy 1978; Smircich and Morgan 1982). Pfeffer (1981: 4) holds that this is the task of management, although it is not easy since people bring with them norms, values and expectations from the larger society into the organisation. Weick (1979b) goes so far as to refer to placebo effects in the sense that it is not essential for us to understand why things work, but only for the participants to believe that they do. In this sense the labels employed by managers when they talk, if they correspond to an organisational body of jargon which in its turn corresponds to a more general popular managerial discourse, might give associations similar to placebo pills used in medicine.

Consequently it seems reasonable to see organisational talk as embedded in the general managerial discourse. If this talk clearly represents the institutionalised norms in the general discourse, then it is more likely to acquire legitimacy. In other words, the general managerial discourse may act as a symbol which contributes to the creation of meaning in local organisational processes. However, the meaning attributed to standards in the popular discourse in these local settings is individual, and could be anything which makes sense of the unknown ambiguous past, present or future.

## Standards and the construction of organisations

Above it has been argued that standards in the popular managerial discourse can be seen as related to organisations insofar as they contribute to the construction of local organisational discourses. It was also argued that it may work as a symbol for meaning and legitimacy when managerial manifestations that represent popular management models are used in talk locally. If the general discourse prompts local organisational discourses, it probably also contributes to the social construction of local thinking on management and organisations, i.e. local organisational paradigms (cf. Pfeffer 1981). For instance, the ways in which individuals think and talk about reality are, according to Weick (1979a), strongly connected with the choices they make and the actions they perform. A similar argument is presented by Ingersoll and Adams (1992) when they discuss children's literature as a major contributor to the creation of our 'meaning maps' through which we observe and interpret the world. However, since people do not cease to create meaning maps when childhood ends, the widespread 'adult' literature on management may very well be an important element of the continuous process of re-creation of individual and collective meaning maps.

In this regard it might be appropriate to describe the general managerial discourse as a framework which contributes to the development of individual meaning maps, or paradigms if we use Pfeffer's (1981) terminology, through which individuals and collectives see the world of management and leadership. By consciously and unconsciously relating their observations and interpretations to these maps, they assess the meaning of different events and representations. In other words, their view of the world has consequences for the way they interpret and judge patterns and representations of the world. This also influences how they translate their observations and interpretations into choices and actions (Weick 1979a).

Consequently, if the general managerial discourse reveals similarities between a few basic assumptions concerning what management and leadership is, then these are likely to be seen as core elements in the meaning maps of many people and local collective paradigms. What is judged as meaningful management may therefore be compared with the standardised view of a manager in the popular discourse, where he or she is presented as omnipotent since a 'good' manager has the 'right' visions, strategies and plans, makes the 'right' decisions, implements the 'right' culture, values and structure; and thereby controls or guides the development of the organisation in the 'right' way to a successful and healthy future.

This suggests that organisations are constructed through talk, thoughts and symbolism. What an organisation is thereby becomes subjective and a result of collective cognitive processes. Weick (1979b: 42) argues, for instance, that an organisation 'is a body of thoughts thought by thinking thinkers'. As argued here, this statement could be complemented by also stating that organisations are sets of talk, talked by talking talkers, and sets of symbols, symbolised by symbolising symbolisers. In this respect an organisation can be described as a cognitive process continuously thought, talked about and symbolised by its members, and one which only exists as long as they keep on doing this collectively. The popular managerial discourse provides these three constructive tools: a legitimate language, legitimate meanings and legitimate symbols that can be used in order to manage meanings (cf. Brunsson and Sahlin-Andersson 1998). By using talk and symbols that are regarded as legitimate by a collective it is possible to manage meanings in local organisations in order to construct a body of thoughts thought by thinking thinkers. This is, however, not an easy task, and copying standards in the discourse is very often problematic and not likely to happen. Instead, it is local translations of these standards that become elements in processes of local organisational construction.

## The popular managerial discourse: a textualised paradise

The purpose of this study is to analyse how popular managerial manifestations are made and what they mean for organisations. The underlying aim can thereby be defined as an attempt to 'look' both behind and at the surface (the rhetoric) of the popular managerial discourse. It could be argued that we have discovered that popular management books of the kind studied here, due to their uniformity and ideological rhetoric, can be seen as edifying literature for management ideologies. In this regard – since business-oriented consultants usually write the most popular texts, and the popular texts are often connected with the activities of consulting firms – it might be appropriate to compare the authors of these books with the medieval crusaders who physically diffused Christianity throughout the world. They claimed to be sent by God, and when the power of the word did not suffice they resorted to the power of the sword. Consultants work mainly with the power of the word, albeit not on a mission from God, and they can be said to advocate assent to a faith in North American managerialism (that the destiny of organisations is a function of management's behaviour) as the best way to paradise. Similar remarks are made by Kostera (1995) who writes that American consultants undertook a 'crusade' in Eastern Europe after the fall of the Iron Curtain. Another point is made by Kinch (1993), who says that it might be appropriate to compare popular management with faith rather than science. Moreover Engwall (1992) raises the question of business administration as a 'modern Latin'. This point is developed further by Furusten and Kinch (1992), who write that this new Latin is American-dominated, but consists of different dialects, i.e. it consists both of the mainstream and its most influential criticism. Nevertheless, the practical implication of this faith and 'modern Latin' could be described in the following way.

Life on the field of battle where business operates is disquieting. Many things are happening at once, and it is very difficult to see obvious relations between actions and results. Participants can really know only a few facts: that decisions must be made and actions must be taken, and that they have to communicate with others about what they are doing. However, which decisions and actions are 'right'? In many situations in business life there are tight schedules and moves must be made rapidly. This means that there is seldom time to carry out systematic investigations. Consequently, practitioners have very little time for contemplation (cf. Carlzon 1951 [1991]; Stewart 1967; Mintzberg 1973) and are therefore likely to turn to their informal allies and to stay in the practical and popular discourse searching for ideas. There they probably find the answers they seek, since those who engage in the discourse are their allies who articulate institutionalised norms and myths. Nevertheless, this does not mean that it will be the best way, or the most successful. But the explanation of organisational events in a language ('modern Latin') which is used by many others, and especially by men who are regarded as learned (like the most famous management 'gurus') may show credibility. This may indicate that what is happening in a particular organisation cannot be completely wrong, since the same process is said to have occurred in other organisations. Nevertheless, no one can be sure that it really has happened anywhere! This also has parallels with religion. For example, no one can prove that Jesus did what the holy book says he did. The strategy of the Catholic church has been impressive in this regard, since (until recently) it spoke of these uncertain events in a language that no one used in ordinary life. To talk in Latin had become part of ceremony and ritual. Even more impressive is that the existence of these rituals was of great importance for billions of people throughout the world. Thus to talk in ritual and ceremonial language may give meaning to activities carried out by specific organisations. In some social networks, genuine Latin still represents this language; in others, managerial Latin may furnish a similar credibility.

One of the major arguments in this study has concerned the standardisation of the popular managerial discourse. This standardisation is believed to be important for organisations, since many organisations and individuals spend large amounts of money to keep in touch with changes in the popular discourse. But does this mean that standardisation in practice will ensue as well? If it does, then there should be only one way to run a business properly, and all organisations should do this since otherwise they will fail. Concerning the practical application of dominating perspectives in the managerial discourse, several studies point out that the public sector endeavours to imitate private corporations and to apply their ideas in their own organisational settings (e.g. Czarniawska-Joerges 1992a; Hasselbladh 1995; Fernler 1996; Forsell and Jansson 1999). However, these endeavours will not mean that their physical actions will be identical. This may lead to the fulfilment of mental expectations while the actual behaviour continues as before (Brunsson 1989). It may also happen that standards are translated, partly or in combination with other standards, into actions. The correspondence with other versions of the same idea may, however, not be particularly significant.

To conclude, this means that the best way to success need not be to imitate the 'good' role models in practice. It might be better to depart from organisation-specific settings and then find new ideas, new destinations and new means of transport. But in so doing it is often more practical to talk in the dominating jargon of the general managerial discourse. In other words, to talk about organisational complexity and ambiguity in the terminology of 'modern ideological Latin' might give credibility and meaning to complex relations which would otherwise be experienced as chaotic. This might be practical in the short run. However, when trying to be practical in the long term it is important to consider the findings in this study, namely that the arguments of the popular managerial discourse tend to be ideological and therefore do not really represent knowledge.

## This is not the end …

The empirical observations reported here concerning the production of popular management books are based on a limited selection of texts, and only one context in which popular books are produced was studied in detail. Therefore the conclusions drawn here about the general characteristics of their production must be seen as indications, not as comprehensive empirical evidence. The major reason for the omission of further empirical data is that this kind of study is rare in the field of management and organisation studies, and much effort in this study had therefore to be devoted to developing methods and a frame of reference whereby related complexities could be discussed. Besides, the aim here was to study the production in detail, which is time-consuming. However, with this study as point of departure, a good suggestion for future research would be to analyse the production of more books or other kinds of managerial manifestations in a similar way. Thus the general validity of the conclusions indicated here could be tested, and a more comprehensive picture of the characteristics of the popular managerial discourse would be acquired.

This is an important research field since, as discussed throughout this study, there seems to be an interaction between the production, diffusion and consumption of popular managerial manifestations. By making more empirical studies of these processes it might be possible to verify what has been indicated here, i.e. that consumption governs production and diffusion. Thereby it could also be argued more convincingly that the producers, distributors, buyers and commentators of popular managerial manifestations are allies. Further studies might also verify our conclusion that there is little room in the popular discourse for those who deliver perspectives other than those held by the allies, and that consequently, scholars who question the boundaries of the popular managerial discourse are not allowed to speak on the popular scene.

If this holds true, we could determine whether scholars who reach theoretical conclusions which contradict the allies are wrong, or raise irrelevant questions, or whether the allies really hold a view of an ideal world? Furthermore, if the allies prefer ideology, this could indicate that they judge knowledge as being of little practical use. It would also mean that the diffusion of 'knowledge', e.g. from academic discourse to practice, is rare. It might even be that academic knowledge is never put into practice if it is not packaged in the terms and forms of the popular discourse. This raises the question of the complexity of the popularisation of knowledge. Will it lose its stringency and reliability when popularised, or is it possible to transform knowledge into simpler, more attainable forms? In this regard, empirical observations of the production, diffusion and consumption of different kinds of managerial manifestations would help us to understand more about the role played in modern society by activities pursued within the academic, practical, political and popular managerial discourse. Thus we might be able to draw conclusions about how knowledge and ideology in management can be distinguished. It might also be possible to discern the roles which, say, organisational and managerial practice, consultancy, politics, journalism and science play in organisational processes on the one hand, and for the development and diffusion of management knowledge on the other. By the same token it would also be appropriate to initiate a discussion of what questions should be investigated in academic research – those which are demanded by practitioners or politicians, or those which are not, but which are believed to be important by academic researchers?

If more empirical data could be collected on the relations between production, diffusion and consumption of managerial manifestations, it would be possible to contribute further to the sociology of knowledge and to the new institutionalism. To date there have been few such studies. But with such a base we could draw more generally verified conclusions on what kind of managerial manifestations practitioners demand, why they demand them, and what these manifestations mean for organisational processes. In this way we would acquire more information on the relations between organisational processes and the managerial discourse as an element of the organisational environment, and on what premises different kinds of manifestations are based. It would thereby also be possible to draw empirically based conclusions about the social forces to which the managerial discourse appeals, and how it affects organisations' situations and thereby the limits to what organisations can do.

The present book only touches on this broad and important research field, but a study has to start somewhere. When this study was initiated in the late 1980s, the area reported on here was wholly unexplored by students of organisations. Over the years a number of studies dealing with the same subject have been published, and there are quite a few in production. Consequently, the major contribution of this and other pioneering work might be that future studies in this field now at least have a basis from which to start.

# Appendix
## Methods of studying the diffusion and production of managerial manifestations

### A pragmatic approach

As pointed out in this book, few studies have hitherto focused on the production and diffusion of managerial knowledge and even fewer deal with popular media. Nor has much attention been paid to the general managerial discourse: particularly not as an element of an organisation's institutional environment. Consequently, there are few studies in the field of organisation and management studies to follow, so that it was necessary to find pragmatic ways to progress. Seeing the research problem from a pragmatic point of view may sometimes be the only way to proceed. Nevertheless, the decision on research strategies and methods is a dilemma which all researchers encounter, and Morgan (1983: 370) describes this very clearly:

> different research strategies do different things, and ... as far as their contributions and knowledge claims are concerned, we should follow Feyerabend (1975) and conclude that 'anything goes'.

By quoting Feyerabend, Morgan would emphasise that different research strategies contribute in different ways, and that it is not possible to determine their validity in any absolute sense. Thus every research strategy may have something to offer, since it may generate information and insights which could not be achieved without using complementary or contradictory methods (Morgan 1983: 380). In this sense, no idea is incapable of improving our knowledge. A more extreme point in this respect is suggested by Wilson (1983) when he postulates the need for an 'anti-method'. He says that methods, or research practices, in social science are often regarded as means of acquiring knowledge. In this sense they can be seen as forms of social interaction (*ibid.*: 247). He proposes that we should not be ready to accept the superiority of improving new knowledge by using certain methods. It may well be that in social science new knowledge is more likely to be obtained in studies carried out in anti-methodological modes, i.e. by trying methods other than those commonly used in the discipline. A reference to the argument in Chapter 3 concerning management studies as a commonplace discipline with no particular core of knowledge, nor any standardised battery of knowledge, supports this argument; so does the argument of McCloskey (1986) who, in a similar way to Wilson (1983), writes that methodologies can be seen as forms of rhetoric. He maintains that methodology, for instance, tells an economist what to do to collect data and how to analyse it. Methodologies also 'help' the researcher to write 'scientific prose' and are often regarded as a toolkit for pursuing scientific research and composing scientific reports (*ibid.*: 24). His point is that rhetoric is the art of speaking, of persuasion; and methodologies as forms of rhetoric indicate what we actually do when we produce information on different topics in writing or in talk.

If we stress this perspective on forms of argument in social science, the validity of improving knowledge by using certain methods will become doubtful, particularly if we follow McCloskey's argument that what is usually judged as good science is on a par with what is meant by good conversation. So, if methodology is indeed a form of argument, then we should judge different arguments according to whether they actually convince different audiences. However, it is difficult to articulate what persuasive rhetoric really is. McCloskey writes, for instance, that a good rhetorician cannot write down his rules since they change over time and between situations (1986: 29). Nevertheless, by searching for the rhetorical characteristics of written or verbal argument, it may be possible to identify general aspects which authors use to persuade their readers. Whether readers really are persuaded, however, is another question.

McCloskey discusses the conditions in the scientific field of economics. His main argument against undue reliance on the trustworthiness of a science which applies predestined methods, is that methodologies of collecting, analysing and presenting data pretend to know how knowledge is to be achieved and articulated before the nature of the knowledge sought is known. He comments on this dilemma in the following terms (*ibid.*: 53):

No one can know what the scientific future will bring: it may be that the centralized, bureaucratized, methodized science that threatens to make the scientists into crank-turners, despite the evidence from the history of science that progress in science is seldom advanced and often retarded by such structure, is just the ticket for the twenty-first century.

He goes on to say that one can do whatever is good for science now, and let the gods decide what is good in the future. This maxim is difficult to fulfil, but he clarifies his argument by saying that good science is practised by good scientists. So, his recipe for making 'good' science is not that scientists must follow certain methodological rules, but is rather to allow 'good' scientists to practice the kind of science of which they are capable, and not to judge their results from the point of view of their skill in using of certain methods. His point is that science does not only advance by using sophisticated formulas or applying well established methods. He means rather 'that science advances by healthy conversation, not adherence to a methodology' (174).

Following the discussions above, the research strategy applied in this study can be defined as pragmatic.[1] Thus it has been pursued step by step, where different methods and principles have been tried. This means that the results of each step helped define the next step. Consequently, this study has not been carried out by following any predestined methodology and model. Instead the data were collected from several sources and by different methods. This is mainly because the object in focus (the general managerial discourse where popular books are selected as representations) is an unorthodox topic in the field of management and organisation studies.

The research process can also be characterised as inductive, since the current findings guided the next step, concerning both empirical observations and theoretical discussions. Nevertheless, each move was prompted by methodological considerations, mainly from what Bryman (1989: 250) classifies as Paradigm II, in which he includes work in a qualitative and interpretative mode (by Paradigm I he means quantitative, functionalist and positivist approaches). According to Burrel and Morgan's (1979) classification of scientific paradigms, this study belongs to the interpretative paradigm. So, this is primarily a qualitative study where interpretation of data is the main procedure of analysis, even though quantitative data are used.[2]

## Studying the diffusion of management books

This study seeks to perform detailed analyses of managerial texts. However, as the supply of management books is so abundant it is not possible to study them all. In this respect texts which are widely distributed can be identified and their authors seen as more significant spokespersons of the general discourse than those who reach a smaller readership. In other words, due to their popularity the authors of these books can be regarded as opinion leaders, fact builders (Latour 1987), or policy makers (DiMaggio and Powell 1983 [1991]), and their texts as significant 'voices' in the general discourse. With this in mind, patterns in the diffusion of books are investigated in this study to enable the identification of significant spokespersons, followed by the selection of a few significant texts in order to scrutinise their production.[3]

However, to discern the most significant spokesperson, i.e. to prove statistically that one person is more significant than another, is not easy. For instance, it is always difficult to gain access to complete lists of sales statistics from publishing houses; indeed such data may not be available since each book sale is just one transaction in their daily business. There are also problems in defining whether or not a book is to be considered as a management book and from what period the sales should be counted. For instance, if Barley and Kunda (1992) and Husczynski (1993) are right that 'old' ideologies and ideas do not disappear from the general discourse, a book achieving great sales today may not be as prominent in the general managerial discourse as, for example Taylor's book from 1911, Barnard's from 1938 or McGregor's from 1960. Besides, some of the bestsellers in the management book genre, such as biographies of famous businessmen and managers like McCormack (1984), Iacocca (1984) and Geneen (1985) should probably be seen as entertainment rather than as having any influence worthy of note on the agenda of the general managerial discourse.

Consequently it may not be possible to prove statistically who the most significant spokespersons are; but when applying a social constructivist approach to reality (cf. Berger and Luckmann 1967) as in the present study, this is not really a problem. The reason is that the significance of different managerial manifestations is regarded in this perspective as a consequence of their social relativity, i.e. the statistically most significant spokesperson may not be the same as the most significant reference in the general managerial discourse. So, the most appropriate way to discern significant spokespersons of the modern general managerial discourse will not necessarily be to use sophisticated statistical methods. Statistics are useful, but it may be more appropriate to compare data from the diffusion of books via different channels, than to focus only on their sales volumes. Therefore statistics collected from different sources are used in this study, and comparisons are made between data from the diffusion of books in both the popular discourse and the academic. To discern a few spokespersons of particular significance, interpretations will be made instead of applying advanced mathematics. We may thus be able to identify a few significant books which can be used later for a more detailed analysis of how popular books are made.

Huczynski (1993) uses statistical sources when he tries to identify management 'gurus'. Quantitative data are also used by Alvarez (1991) in his study of the diffusion and institutionalisation of organisational knowledge in Britain, Mexico and Spain. Alvarez collected statistics on economic and political crises, and on the diffusion of one concept in formal (business schools) and informal (media and books) education, governmental promotion and in particular business groups. Engwall (1992) also employed quantitative data in his analysis of the origin of literature used over time in teaching at the Stockholm School of Economics. Data of a similar kind are also collected in the present study, first to map general characteristics in the field of managerial texts and then to identify significant spokespersons for these characteristics. We can thereby search for characteristics of the origin of management books in general, but also among the most popular manifestations. To sketch the general view, quantitative data stored in libraries' registers and databases are used to search for characteristics concerning the origin of books, and the yearly increase in the stock of books of different origin. However, to identify a few significant spokespersons, a more detailed stock of books is needed, and the diffusion of books in what we call the popular discourse is studied with this in mind. Therefore the stock of titles supplied by management book clubs, books appearing on a bestseller list in a leading business journal, and sales statistics from leading publishing houses are investigated. To obtain a broader view of the general significance of voices in the popular discourse, a comparison is conducted with one channel belonging to the academic discourse, namely the diffusion of books used in teaching at Swedish universities and university colleges.

To sum up, by considering the characteristics of the diffusion of books through these different channels we can discern general characteristics of the origin of books. Thereafter, by focusing on a more detailed population of books, a few significant spokespersons can be identified who represent characteristics both on the general level and in the narrower populations. To discern the significance of these persons, patterns in the different distribution channels will be interpreted. In so doing the aim is not to single out the most significant 'voices' in the general managerial discourse, but rather to identify a few spokespersons who represent significant characteristics of management books that become popular. Then a few books written by these spokespersons can be selected for more detailed analyses of the contents and production of the texts.

## Studying the production of management texts

Latour (1987) suggests two ways to study the production of texts, or if we use his words, to reopen black boxes and discover what lies within. One is to enter the text and analyse its content and rhetoric to see what is built into it, i.e. the hidden agenda (55); the other to enter the context where it is produced, or in Latour's words, to 'sneak into the places where the papers are written and to follow the construction of facts in their most intimate details' (63). By so doing we can study the motives, considerations, and social forces surrounding the production and diffusion of managerial texts.

This approach is close to what Wilson (1983) and McCloskey (1986) mean with their suggestion of an anti-methodology. Using Latour's (1987) terms, the object is scrutinised from the outside, i.e. by applying other methods than those used in the original texts. It is thereby possible to study how texts, and thereby managerial manifestations, are created.[4]

### Entering texts[5]

In a study of how organisational texts can be interpreted, Kets de Vries and Miller (1987) advocate an anthropological approach and discuss three particular strategies. The first searches for central themes and patterns, ideas or sentiments which constitute the 'surface' of the text and often appear to explain many consequences. The second searches for elements which have deep, perhaps unconscious, emotional significance. This can also be defined as affective components motivating a text or characterising the dialogue therein. Their third strategy is a process where the initial interpretations are tested against others' interpretations of reality. In what follows we discuss Kets de Vries and Miller's first and second strategies as an initial step in characterising the text, since they both focus on the surface. Their third strategy is discussed as a second step, called textual deconstruction, where the aim is to go beyond the surface. However, after having characterised the contents and deconstructed the surface of the text, the question remains of what the text represents according to the conclusions drawn in steps one and two. Can any specific characteristic be identified? As a third step, we determine whether the texts represent knowledge or ideology.

*Characterising texts (step one)*

Following Kets de Vries and Miller, it is appropriate to start the process by identifying the main themes and issues stressed in the text. This requires a careful reading where a search for patterns can be carried out in an ethnographic mode. In other words an open approach is applied where patterns are sought for rather than a predestined model followed. The patterns found can then be used as points of departure for further analysis.

The same approach (i.e. the search for patterns) can be used when looking for rhetorical characteristics. However, Kets de Vries and Miller's (1987) methodological discussion is quite brief and general. A more elaborate discussion of how texts can be analysed is offered by Czarniawska-Joerges (1988). She studied the language (talk) used by management consultants and emphasised language and rhetorical skills as important aspects of what they do. For instance, she calls them 'salesmen in words' and one of her conclusions is that consultants often traffic in labels and metaphors when presenting their ideas, solutions and opinions. According to Czarniawska-Joerges, texts can be characterised by three linguistic artefacts, namely labels, metaphors and platitudes, which she defines as follows (Czarniawska-Joerges 1993: 19):

> Labels tell us *what* things are; they classify ('this is a cost'). Metaphors say *how* things are (what they are like); they create images ('cash cows', 'competitive edges'). Platitudes establish what is *normal*; they conventionalize ('all that can go wrong will')

For Czarniawska-Joerges, the concept 'label' means what names things are given. When studying a text it is possible to analyse how labels are used and whence they come. Do authors, for instance, use concepts like strategy, goals, corporate culture, decentralisation and visions as if they have taken-for-granted meanings? Do they use them as labels, or do they give detailed explanations and definitions of these concepts? If so, what sources do they use to make their argument credible? By raising these questions about a text it is possible to observe and search for patterns therein and thereby characterise it in terms of how labels appear, i.e. whether the author is likely to 'drop' many concepts, or if he or she gives detailed explanations.

The appearance of metaphors in a text can be studied in the same way, i.e. are metaphors likely to be used to strengthen the argument or to make the point more precise? For example, it may happen that accounts of extreme situations and events in successful companies, or the behaviour of famous entrepreneurs and managers, are used by the authors as metaphors to illustrate why a certain kind of behaviour is 'good' and another 'bad'. Czarniawska-Joerges (1988: 22–3) says that metaphors are 'creating new significations [and] reducing the insecurity caused by meeting what is new; they are relating to something more recognizable than the object of the metaphor'. This indicates the function of a metaphor, i.e. what effect metaphors might have on the reader of a text. However, in the present study we shall not comment on the function of texts. Instead the focus is limited to the degree that metaphors feature in the argument.

Platitudes can also be mapped in this way. As defined by Czarniawska-Joerges (1988: 29) platitudes represent what is normal. Furthermore, the concept of platitude can be used to represent an argument which resembles conclusions based on bald statements. This is similar to an author drawing conclusions from labels or metaphors without explaining their meaning and underlying assumptions. It does not mean that statements are 'wrong', or 'false' representations of reality, but rather that the author uses a statement as a fact upon which he or she bases further discussions and conclusions. One example of such an argument is when the statement 'the leadership style that the founder of IBM had was visionary and open' is used as the basis of the conclusion 'therefore companies need visionary and open leaders'. Platitudinous argument is thereby a rhetorical feature which can characterise texts.

By using these linguistic artefacts, Czarniawska-Joerges (1988) characterises the parlance of consultants. Thus she examines the extent to which consultants use labels, metaphors, and platitudes to explain what they mean, or the extent to which their talk can be characterised as detailed explanations of what the concepts employed mean. The use of the linguistic artefacts as rhetorical categories is a possible strategy in making characterisations of the rhetoric in management books. The underlying method of so doing is to observe, and interpret what is observed. However, a problem inherent in this method is that the interpretations are the researcher's and are therefore not objective. It is thereby difficult to control the credibility of such interpretations. Thus the only way to tell the reader how interpretations are made in this study is to describe the considerations and approaches which provoked them.

*Deconstructing texts (step two)*

The characterisation of its 'surface', i.e. the search for tendencies in main issues and rhetoric, gives one a picture of the text. However, if we would understand what texts represent as environmental elements, it is important to determine whether there is something beneath the surface, i.e. whether it contains a 'hidden' message. This is discussed by Cooper (1986) when he introduces deconstruction as a way to decompose the surface of a text. This means that we look beyond the surface in search of hidden but underlying arguments. However, according to Cooper, deconstruction is not one specific method, but should be seen as an approach to a text.[6] The study of texts as discussed above as a first step means, according to Cooper, that we characterise only their 'surface'. In other words we identify the main issues and rhetorical characteristics, while 'deconstructing' a text means going 'beyond the surface', i.e. searching for what Latour (1987) calls a 'hidden agenda'.

In this respect different strategies have been applied in earlier studies. For instance, Calàs and Smircich (1991) analyse how texts distinguish between other terms or definitions in other texts. They compare texts by Barnard (1938), Mintzberg (1973) and Peters and Waterman (1982) with feminist texts, and conclude that the management books on which they focus can be seen as seductive. This practice resembles what Kets de Vries and Miller (1987) call a process where the initial interpretations are tested against others' interpretations of reality. They hold that one interpretation of how an organisation works must be related to other interpretations of the same process. However, when studying management books, this method needs to be adjusted, and one way so to do is to compare the interpretation of a book with interpretations made by others. Published reviews of particular books could be used for this purpose, or individuals could be commissioned to produce reviews, then these reviews could be analysed to see whether there are similarities in the reviewers' opinions of the texts.[7] However, since there can never be one reading of a text (cf. Giddens 1979) it is always possible that someone else will arrive at a different interpretation. In other words, this would probably not bring us closer to the 'true' interpretation.

Nor do we intend to find the 'true' interpretation. Instead we shall search for underlying, taken-for-granted, 'hidden' arguments in the text. This is discussed by Kilduff (1993: 15–16) who performs a deconstructive reading of a text to 'challenge' its surface by asking such questions as:

Why are certain authors, topics, or schools excluded from the text? Why are certain themes never questioned, whereas other themes are condemned? Why, given a set of premises, are certain conclusions not reached? The aim of such questions is not to point out textual errors but to help the reader to understand the extent to which the text's objectivity and persuasiveness depend on a series of strategic exclusions.

In particular this involves a displacement of taken-for-granted meanings of a certain argument and an exploitation of the possibilities of other meanings (cf. Burrell and Cooper 1988). This approach seems fruitful for the present study. To develop a deconstructive strategy it therefore seems appropriate to start from the results of the analyses in the first step, i.e. the main issues and the rhetorical characteristics. A few major themes can thereby be identified around which the argument in the text circles. In other words the line of argument of a few major 'part' discussions in the text can be selected for scrutiny, and searched for taken-for-granted meanings which are not explained or questioned. In this way it is possible to analyse the basic assumptions on which the argument of the text rests. For instance, we can determine whether it is founded on knowledge, beliefs, myths, institutions or ideologies. Or we can search for the origin of the arguments upon which the rhetoric of the text is founded.

Again, as in the first step, the findings from such a textual deconstruction depend on the researcher's own interpretations. Thus the criticism raised in the previous paragraph is also relevant here.

*Studying what texts represent: knowledge or ideology? (step three)*

The results of the analyses in steps one and two yield a third step in defining what a text represents. Chapter 3 commented on how textualisations in the general managerial discourse of the patterns in the world system may be parts of institutional mechanisms in organisations' environments which carry representations of managerial practice between organisations and societies. Such representations can differ in character, i.e. they can be defined as knowledge, ideologies, beliefs, myths or institutions. In this regard it can be argued that dominant 'voices' in the general managerial discourse might 'serve' local organisational processes with such representations. If we would understand this relationship between management books as important 'voices' in the general managerial discourse and local organisational processes, it is therefore crucial to discover what a text represents. This is significant, since organisations can be seen as embedded in systems of knowledge, beliefs, myths, institutions and ideologies (Scott and Meyer 1983; 1991; Meyer 1994). This also pertains to local organisational settings, since managerial work can be seen as controlling and maintaining myths, images, symbols and labels (Weick 1979b).

To characterise the content of dominant 'voices' in the general discourse in terms of whether they represent knowledge or ideology is therefore one way to determine how the general discourse is related to local organisational processes. Thus, due to the ambiguous, and subtle, characters of these concepts (cf. Chapter 2) it is important to note that the concepts are not used here to qualify whether a specific line of thought is 'true' and thereby represents 'real knowledge', and others are 'false' and thereby represent ideology. Instead, the approach applied here sees these concepts as characteristics of different kinds of argumentation, i.e. particular ways to organise an oral or written text. Thus it is not the meaning of an argument which is at issue here; instead, the focus is on characterising its rhetoric. This may be unorthodox, but it is one way to analyse what dominant 'voices' in the general managerial discourse represent.

The reason for developing a framework consisting of two extremes, knowledge and ideology, is that it is thereby possible to characterise what the rhetoric of a text represents as an environmental element. As a next step, the influence of texts on organisational processes can be discussed theoretically. Such analysis is rare, and earlier institutional studies give little help.

However, using knowledge (cognitive rhetoric) and ideology (ideological rhetoric) as two ideal types is not unproblematic since their meanings are subtle and often biased. Besides, there is also the dimension that the meaning of the one or the other concept is judged by their social relativity in different contexts (cf. Berger and Luckmann 1967). Nevertheless, by starting from the analyses in the first and second steps, a third step can be to analyse the rhetoric with regard to the extent to which it can be characterised as drawing upon personal experience, myths, beliefs and institutions.[8] The greater the content of these concepts, the more ideological the text, and vice-versa. Another aspect is the degree to which the text is positioned to other studies – do the authors 'cross' paths (Latour 1987: 220) taken by others (confront and position the texts to supporting or contradictory studies) or are they more likely to avoid references or take others' paths (i.e. only refer to a mainstream of studies in passing)? The higher the degree of crossing paths, the more an argument can be seen as mobile, stable, and combinable (Latour 1987: 223) and thereby as more appropriate to be characterised as representing knowledge.

To do this in practice, a text can be analysed in detail concerning how references are used in the argument. In this respect the definition of the rhetoric, in terms of metaphors, platitudes and labels as suggested in step one above, is useful in providing a point of departure. The patterns thus identified then allow interpretations of the extent to which a text's argument can be said to draw on beliefs, myths and institutions, and thereby represents cognitive or ideological rhetoric. According to the definitions in this section concerning how a text can be said to be either cognitive or ideological, it can be argued that the higher the degree of impersonal argument, crossing other people's paths, and systematism, the higher the degree of cognitive rhetoric. On the other hand, the higher the degree of personal argument, presence of beliefs, myths and institutions in combination with normative claims in explaining complex relations, the higher the degree of ideological rhetoric. These two definitions indicate two extreme types of rhetoric. However, in a scientific field like management studies, where scholars create manifestations of management and deal in commonsense (cf. Whitley 1984a: 90–1), this might be rare with pure cognitive or ideological texts. Further, when the decision on whether a manifestation represents ideology or knowledge can be said to be based on its social relativity in different social networks (cf. Berger and Luckmann 1967), manifestations produced by both academic researchers and many management consultants are likely to be a mixture of ideological and cognitive rhetoric. However, it seems reasonable to stress that academic researchers are most likely to deal with a higher degree of cognitive rhetoric, while consultants are more inclined to use ideological rhetoric. Nevertheless, this is an empirical question on which this study will shed some light.

*Examining the context of production*

Searching for characteristics of the production process

To obtain a comprehensive view of the production of texts and what they represent in society it may be useful, as Latour (1987: ch. 2) suggests, to study not only texts, but also the organisational context in which they are created. The aim of examining a text in this way is to search for motives, considerations and social forces in the process behind and surrounding the production of particular texts. Latour recommends an ethnographic approach to the fabrication of scientific facts and technical artefacts, where the researcher follows and observes the scientists and engineers (Latour's concern is technoscience) at the times and places where they plan and create the final product. In brief, Latour suggests that the researcher should enter the place where the author works (the context) and make observations and ask questions; by so doing it is possible to be at the location where a text is produced before it is packaged by the author into a black box. Being there beforehand makes it possible to study an author's motives, considerations and prototypes.

One problem in carrying out such studies relates to when and where the texts in focus are produced. We can here distinguish between texts which have been produced, which are in production, and which will be produced. If the text in focus is one of the last two kinds, it is then possible to follow Latour's suggestion of actually observing the production process. But if the text is of the first kind then we need to re-construct the production process. The most obvious way of doing this is to interview significant actors who were involved in the process. Another method is to read and analyse other documents and books produced in the same context during the same period. Yet another is to collect statistics on the organisation's development, and the environmental development to which the context belongs. By so doing, a 'text' of the context can be produced. So, by compiling a selection of observable texts of the context, both already written, as well as transcripts from interviews, a new, broader story of the context underlying popular texts and their production can be told.

It is not possible to study a popular book in its production, since one cannot tell before the event whether or not a book will be popular. Therefore it is most appropriate to study the production of popular management books by following the reconstruction strategy. With this in mind, data are in this study collected through interviews, a selection of statistics, and analyses of other texts produced in the context.

All data on the context were collected and analysed in an ethnographic mode, where the aim was to follow the development of a representative context in which popular management books are produced. In this regard, interest was explicitly directed towards processes of creation of a 'body of knowledge' upon which the specific book was based. The questions put to respondents were in this sense open, meaning that they were free to give their view of the development of the context. The interviews were not taped, since such methods sometimes create an uncomfortable atmosphere. Instead careful notes were taken, and some of the interviews were held together with one of the co-authors of the first report on the production process. Each interview was thereafter written down, and analysed as a text. Patterns were sought in the same way as when we examined texts in order to study their main issues (see above). Other texts produced within the same context were similarly studied.

## An analytical scheme

When patterns in the context have been sought it may be appropriate to apply an analytical scheme to further the analysis. Therefore we shall here discuss general variations between different contexts of production in the academic, popular, practical and political discourse. Nevertheless, it is important to point out that the data in this study were not collected with the scheme developed here as point of departure. Instead, as discussed above, data were collected and analysed in an ethnographic mode, and the scheme is a result of these analyses. This means in particular that the dimensions of production of managerial manifestations discussed here emanate from the patterns found on examining the context in which a single popular management book was produced. As described in Chapter 6, four major dimensions are: research orientation, business orientation, concentration and standardisation. Consequently, these are used below to illustrate how they tend to link up and how they are related to contexts of production in different discourses.

The contexts in which managerial texts are produced can vary widely due to specifics in different discourses, i.e. the practices of academic researchers, management consultants, business journalists and practising managers are different and have different foci and requisites. For instance, these contexts differ in terms of research orientation. This is discussed here taking into account such factors as an author's academic affiliation and previous scientific publications. In other words, we asked to what degree could the process of creation of knowledge be characterised as 'crossing other people's paths' (cf. Latour 1987: 220), i.e. oriented to other studies. A high degree of this implied a strong research orientation, and vice-versa. However, the relevance of these paths also needs to be considered. Other features of research orientation are a high degree of systematism, continuous communication, and of scrutiny of the material. This means that the label 'research orientation' is used here in a similar sense to cognitive rhetoric, when we discussed how texts could be characterised. The difference is that when we analyse the context of production we study motives, considerations and social forces (again, Latour 1987) in the process which yields a published book. Research in the academic discourse is likely to score high regarding research orientation, since researchers are expected to cross paths and write scientific reports if they want to be accepted in the discourse. On the other hand, actions in the popular discourse, where journalism is probably the most extreme medium, is liable to score low, since journalists' acceptance derives from their ability to raise interesting questions and pursue exciting issues. However, actions within the practical and political discourse usually score low in research orientation. This does not mean that only academics act systematically, but that academic affiliation and scientific publication are activities which are rare in discourses other than the academic.

Business orientation is another dimension where there are likely to be differences in the activities within different discourses, and can be related to Collins' (1979) discussion of the commercialisation of knowledge. We use it here to assess the degree of ethics in business, i.e. whether profits earned from selling 'knowledge' are used to develop new knowledge, or to improve the position on the market. The judgement of the output, i.e. the judgement of the managerial manifestations offered on the market, is also considered. Is it controlled by colleagues within the profession – i.e. do consultants, for example, judge each other's performance – or by an external committee such as academia, or is the quality assessed by the consumers, i.e. those who buy the manifestations?[9] In this regard, activities in the academic discourse, such as research and university teaching, are more likely to score low in business orientation since by tradition they are not sold on the market. On the other hand, activities within the popular discourse such as journalism and consultancy score high in this regard since the idea is to sell newspapers and advice. Activities within the practical and political discourse probably also score low, since the idea here is not primarily to sell managerial manifestations. However, practitioners are involved in the consultants' business since they buy what consultants offer.

There are also hybrids of the popular and the academic discourse which combine activities belonging to both and carry out 'action-research' or 'clinical-research'. This means that consultancy commissions are designed as research projects, i.e. as a strategy to finance research and to collect data (e.g. Greiner and Metzger 1983; Schein 1988; Gummesson 1991). Opinions differ on whether or not such a mix is successful for the development of management knowledge. Gummesson (1991) therefore states, for example, that it is often the best way to carry out relevant research and develop relevant knowledge, while Engwall *et al.* (1993 [1997]) argue that it seems to be most liable to contribute to both research and practice (through consultancy) if such activities are pursued in a specialised area on a specialised topic where there are few competitors in operation. Above all, the major complexity concerns whether the context in which managerial manifestations are created is characterised as making business out of knowledge, i.e. where those who buy control the quality, or whether there is a collective struggle or professional association which sets the standards, or whether academia constitutes the quality control.

Another dimension of developing knowledge is the degree of concentration in the work. This seems to be dependent on the degree of orientation to research or business. However, it is particularly related to Whitley's (1984a: 227–34) analysis of the concept of task uncertainty in different scientific fields, i.e. uncertainty concerning tasks, research problems and methods. He maintains that the greater the uncertainty, the less the concentration in the accumulated struggle in the field. Therefore, the more uncertain and vague the area and topic, the more general the field, and vice-versa. Whitley (1984a: 158) defines the field of management studies as characterised by high task uncertainty and thus low concentration. However, the present study is concerned with the work within one particular organisational context, not the entire field of management studies. Nevertheless, the concept concentration is relevant if used in Whitley's sense. Thus it is suited to discussing the degree of concentration on particular issues, problems and objects in the context. In this regard there is tendency for high concentration to coincide with strong specialisation (i.e. a focus on a few issues, problems and objects) and low concentration with wide generalisation (i.e. a focus on several issues, problems and objects).

Yet another dimension of importance in the production of managerial manifestations is standardisation. This concept was used in earlier chapters when we referred in particular to DiMaggio and Powell's (1983 [1991]) discussion of isomorphic tendencies between organisations operating in the same organisational field. Nevertheless, the approach to this in the present study consists of a detailed examination of a few spokespersons. In this regard standardisation is analysed to see whether the development in the context can be characterised as openness and uniqueness, or uniformity of work methods, body of knowledge, concepts and services supplied. This approach to standardisation in the production of managerial manifestations corresponds to Whitley's (1984a: 31) discussion of the standardisation of work procedures, techniques and methods in different scientific fields to enable control and coordination of outcomes. Consequently, standardisation can be studied on a scale which indicates whether a higher degree of uniqueness means a lower degree of standardisation, and vice-versa.

## Conclusion

This appendix advocates a pragmatic, step-by-step approach to a research object where few prototype studies are to be found. Since texts are not created in a vacuum, it seemed appropriate to start from a study of the supply of management books. For this reason it was suggested that we need to draw up a map of the field of books and select a few significant spokespersons to study the production of popular texts in more detail. It was decided to apply two major strategies in studying contents and production; first to examine the text, and second to examine the context in which a text is produced. The content should be studied in three steps. The first step characterises texts in terms of their background, main issues and rhetorical characteristics (i.e. their surface). The second deconstructs the text into patterns of key discussions, and the third defines what the text represents as an environmental element in terms of knowledge or ideology. To study the process of text's production it is suggested that the context in which it is produced be examined through either ethnographic participating observations, or if a historical process is at issue (as here), to hold interviews with participants in the process and examine other texts and documents produced in the same context. Patterns can then be sought which can later be discussed in relation to other studies of similar phenomena. To this end, an analytical scheme can be applied consisting of four dimensions of the production of a managerial manifestation (research orientation, business orientation, concentration and standardisation).

# Notes

## Chapter 1

1 See also the wrapper of one of the later editions of the book.
2 The six 'families of ideas' Huczynski discusses are: bureaucracy, scientific management, administrative management, human relations, neo-human relations and guru theory. The themes he mentions are the understanding of the work world, status enhancements and practical application. (*ibid.*: ch. 3)
3 An important reference for them is Bendix's (1956) study of managerial ideologies. Perrow's (1986) discussion, which is based mainly on Bendix's work, is also closely related.
4 A detailed discussion of methodological considerations and methods of studying the diffusion and production of popular management books is given in an appendix to this book.
5 See also Atkinson (1990), who presents a discussion similar to that of Latour but from the point of view of sociological texts.

## Chapter 2

1 Whitley (1985) and Alvarez (1991) point out similar fields of activities when they discuss the diffusion of managerial knowledge. Moreover, when Meyer and Rowan (1977; 1991) discuss three origins of rational institutional myths, they also mention similar sources, namely the elaboration of complex relational networks, the degree of collective environmental organisation, and leadership efforts of local organisations.

## Chapter 3

1 For more references with a similar approach to knowledge see Whitley (1984: esp. 273). Other related extensive discussions on knowledge are Kuhn (1970), Burrel and Morgan (1979) and Willmott (1993).
2 For a more detailed and elaborated discussion concerning the two extremes of knowledge and ideology – as used here – see Appendix.
3 For more references to oral and written textualisations of reality, see for instance Ong (1982).

## Chapter 4

1 This chapter is based on Furusten and Kinch (1992).

2 Akademibokhandeln (Mäster Samuelsgatan, Stockholm), East and West (Nybrogatan, Stockholm), Lundequistska (Uppsala), Åkerbloms (Umeå), Affärsbokhandeln (Malmö) and Wettergrens (Göteborg).

3 This figure covers Swedish sales of the Swedish edition of the books published by Swedish publishers Svenska Dagbladet Förlag. This means that sales of the original English version are excluded. Consequently, the real Swedish sales figures are actually larger than indicated here.

4 Interview with Richard Normann.

5 The original study was conducted by one of my students and is presented in Kragelund (1992); a first report including these data is published in Furusten and Kinch (1996).

6 Richard Normann, Lars Bruzelius and Per-Hugo Skärvad were colleagues at the Swedish consulting firm SIAR when the first version of *Integrerad Organisationslära* was published in 1974, and when Normann wrote the first report on what later appeared in the book *Service Management*. This marks the importance of SIAR as a context where books used in higher management education in Sweden are produced.

## Chapter 5

1 Other versions of this chapter have been published elsewhere (Furusten 1993a; 1998).

2 The analyses here are made of Swedish versions of the books, since these have mainly characterised the Swedish managerial discourse; however, the quotations are taken from the English versions.

3 For details of the methodological considerations behind these strategies, see Appendix.

4 As a result of the book's success, the authors have travelled the global lecture circuit ever since. Tom Peters has been most active in this regard, and according to information given to participants at 'The Tom Peters Conference' organised by the *Economist* on 13 February 1990 in London, he gives about 150 lectures and seminars a year worldwide.

5 The analysis is based on two versions of the book: the original Swedish (Normann 1983) and the second Swedish edition (Normann 1991). However, the quotations are taken from the the first version in English (Normann 1984).

6 A 'good' circle arises when there is efficiency in the 'moments of truth', i.e. when management succeeds in bringing about conformity in beliefs, values, philosophy and thereby culture. In a 'bad' circle this does not occur (Normann 1983: 173).

7 The original version of *Service Management* from 1983 comprises 188 pages, and *In Search of Excellence* 368 pages.

## Chapter 6

1 This chapter is based on Engwall *et al.* (1993 [1997]) and Furusten (1993b).

2 After a merger with SIFO (a Swedish polling institute) in 1990, SMG now stands for SIFO Management Group (R4). (Note that the numbers in parentheses, e.g. (R4), refer to the respondents. For reasons of anonymity the numbers do not coincide with the alphabetical list of interviewees presented at the end of this book.)

3 *Vem är Det (Who's Who in Sweden)* 1993.

4 Note that other consulting organisations, such as the Boston Consulting Group (founded in 1963), appeared at the same time (Läckgren *et al.* 1989: 11).

5 *Svenska Dagbladet*, 5 August 1964.

6 *Svenska Dagbladet*, 6 July 1965.

7 Some of the early projects were commissioned by the Department of Commerce and the National Patent and Registration Office (Läckgren *et al.* 1989: 14). Other clients were organisations in the construction industry (R2). In addition, four grants were given by the Social Science Research Council in 1966–7, and one grant from the Bank of Sweden Tercentenary Foundation (archive material). Scholarships were provided by Norrlandsfonden and Marcus and Marianne Wallenberg's Foundation (R4).

8 In 1968, Rhenman published *Organisationsplanering (Organisational Planning)* (1968b), which described a study of organisational consultants. The book was a revised version of a report which had appeared in 1964. In the following year, Rhenman reported on the project at the Eskilstuna Central Hospital (Rhenman 1969a; 1973b) and published a synthesis of long-range planning projects (Rhenman 1969b; 1973a). The latter was to a large extent based on restructuring projects, particularly through divisionalisation, in Swedish companies such as Perstorp, Felix, Husqvarna and Sockerbolaget (R12). For a summary of some of these divisionalisation projects, see Edgren *et al.* (1983). Other team members presented project results in the form of licentiate and doctoral theses (Wallroth 1968; Normann 1969; Olofsson 1969; Sandkull 1970; Stymne 1970). Thus research orientation permeated the organisation. Normann, Olofsson, Sandkull and Stymne have all held chairs (Normann as acting and adjunct professor, the others still hold their chairs).

9 During Rhenman's leave of absence the Harvard professor Larry Bennigson worked with SIAR and the Department of Business Administration at Lund University (R12).

10 *SIAR Alumni Register*.

11 An example of a thesis with such SIAR connections is Danborg *et al.* (1975).

12 From 1973 Normann worked part-time for a few years in the department as Associate Professor (R6).

13 It is worth mentioning that the theoretical framework, the models and conclusions here discussed are the tenets also of his 1983 book *Service Management*. The author himself said that the latter book can be seen in many ways as a popularisation of his dissertation.

14 An important factor in this decision was probably that the consulting activities of HBS professors were far more restricted than Rhenman had experienced in Lund (R4).

15 For the internationalisation process, cf. Sharma 1987: 257–60.

16 Efforts to create sophisticated consulting manuals had been in progress since SIAR Planning was founded in 1970, but a more organised 'strong pull' was taken around 1978–9.

17 Advertising material from SMG.

18 Advertising material from SMG, R6 and R7.

19 Cf. Normann *et al.* 1989: 9; and advertising material from SMG.

20 Cf. also advertising material from SMG.

21 In the mid-1980s McKinsey expanded its efforts in Scandinavia. Earlier these interests had been limited. In a few years they became one of the most popular consultancy firms in Sweden.

22 A well established Swedish research company (polling institute) which had recently created a management consultancy division.

23 Advertising material from SMG.

24 *Svenska Dagbladet*, 6 July 1965.

## Chapter 7

1 The famous managers are: Jan Carlzon (1985; 1987), at the time Managing Director of SAS; Lee Iacocca (1984), former manager at Ford and at the time MD at Chrysler; Christer Ericsson (1987), former MD of Consafe. The consultants are: Peters and Waterman (1982); Blanchard and Johnson (1982); Sveiby and Risling (1986); Karlöf (1985).

2 See Appendix for a detailed definition of what is meant by ideological and cognitive rhetoric in this study.

## Appendix

1 Pragmatism in social research is discussed by Czarniawska-Joerges (1992b: 62).

2 For explicit readings of complexities associated with interpretation see, for instance, Ödman (1979).

3 Latour (1987) refers to significant spokespersons, by which he means those who speak for others who do not speak (*ibid.*: 71). This means that a spokesperson represents both him/herself plus things and people connected to the situation when he/she speaks. Latour's definition is connected to local situations where some persons speak for a group of others and represent their opinions every now and then.

4 See also Atkinson (1990), who presents a discussion similar to that of Latour but from the point of view of sociological texts.

5 This part is based on discussions carried out in Furusten (1992; 1996).

6 Cooper bases his discussion on Jacques Derrida's work and presents a postmodern view of Derrida's contributions to organisation studies.

7 The commissioning of students to review articles in the mass media has been attempted by Chen and Meindl (1991).

8 Myths: according to Giddens (1979: 40–1) a myth has no particular author, and exists only as incarnated in a tradition and is thereby taken for granted as a representative story of this tradition. A similar definition is given by Alvesson and Berg (1988), who say that a myth does not have to be connected to a particular context (like a single corporation), it can be wider and appear in several contexts. It is close to the meaning of sagas, tales and legends, i.e. stories of social order that are very difficult to trace

back to their original context. Thus it is also hard to control a myth's trustworthiness. Whether it is seen as a myth or not depends on its social relativity (cf. Berger and Luckmann 1967: 100).

Beliefs: in this context we mean arguments by individuals or collectives that are believed to represent reality, but whose meaning is not mobile since they are not stable when combined and confronted with other representations. In comparison with knowledge, Latour (1987: 182) writes that beliefs are 'less objective' than knowledge, they are more like 'half truths'. In this regard beliefs can be defined as how individuals and collectives 'want' things to be in certain situations. In this respect it concerns things that are believed as 'almost being known'. Thus if beliefs are not confronted with contradictory arguments, then their meaning in their particular context is likely to remain.

Institutions: according to Berger and Luckmann (1967: 70–85), there are notions which when repeated frequently are taken for granted by individuals in particular social networks, and thereby regarded almost as 'natural' routines of everyday life. Such notions can be called institutions from which people start when they act (Berger and Luckmann 1967: 72; Jepperson 1991). This means that institutions are particularly accepted sets of knowledge, beliefs and myths. Further, according to DiMaggio and Powell (1991b: 8) an institution means standards of behaviour which are 'defined by customs and obligations'. In a similar way Jepperson (1991: 147) writes that institutions become taken for granted in some ways due to their effects on expectations. An institution thereby consists of practices and roles that can easily be identified and that are typical in certain contexts (almost as if they were natural).

9 Cf. also Whitley (1984a; 1984b).

# Bibliography

Abrahamson, E. (1996) 'Technical and Aesthetic Fashion', in B. Czarniawska and G. Sevón (eds) *Translating Organisational Change*, Berlin: de Greuyter, 117–38.

Alvarez, J-L. (1991) 'The International Diffusion and Institutionalization of the New Entrepreneurship Movement: A Study in the Sociology of Knowledge', dissertation, Boston MA: Harvard University.

Alvesson, M. (1989) *Ledning av Kunskapföretaget*, Stockholm: Norstedts.

Argyris, C. and Schön, D. (1978) *Organizational Learning*, Reading MA: Addison-Wesley.

Atkinson, P. (1990) *The Ethnographic Imagination: Textual Constructions of Reality*, London: Routledge.

Bakka, J. and Fivelsdal, E. (1988) *Organisationsteori: Struktur, Kultur, Processer (Organisation Theory: Structure, Culture, Processes)* Stockholm: Liber.

Barley, S. and Kunda, G. (1992) 'Design and Devotion: Surges of Rational and Normative Ideologies of Control in Managerial Discourse', *Administrative Science Quarterly*, 37, 363–99.

Barnard, C. (1938) *The Functions of the Executive*, Cambridge MA: Harvard University Press.

Bendix, R. (1956) *Work and Authority in Industry*, New York: Wiley.

Berger, P. L. and Luckmann, T. (1967) *The Social Construction of Reality*, New York: Penguin.

Björkman, T. (1997) 'Management: en Modeindustri' ('Management: a Fashion Industry') in Å. Sandberg (ed.) *Ledning för Alla (Management for All)* Stockholm: SNS Förlag, 58–85.

Blanchard, K. and Johnson, S. (1982) *The One-Minute Manager*, Englewood Cliffs NJ: Prentice-Hall.

Bloomfield, B. and Best, A. (1992) 'Management Consultants: Systems Development, Power and the Translation of Problems', *The Sociological Review*, 533–59.

Bloomfield, B and Vurdubakis, T. (1994) 'Re-presenting Technology: IT Consultancy Reports as Textual Reality Constructions', *Sociology*, 28, 2, 455–77.

Brunsson, N. (1989) *The Organization of Hypocrisy: Talk, Decision and Actions in Organizations*, Chichester: Wiley.

——(1997) 'The Standardization of Organizational Forms as a Cropping-up Process', *Scandinavian Journal of Management*, 307–20.

Brunsson, N. and Olsen, J. P. (1993) *The Reforming Organization*, New York: Routledge.

Brunsson, N. and Sahlin-Andersson, K., 'Att skapa organisationer' ('Creating Organizations') in G. Ahrne (ed.) *Stater som Organisationer (States as Organisations)* Stockholm: Nerenius & Santérus Förlag, 61–98.

Bruzelius, L. and Skärvad, P-H. (1988) [1974] *Integrerad Organisationslära (Integrated Organisation Theory)* Lund: Studentlitteratur.

Bryman, A. (1989) *Research Methods and Organisation Studies*, London: Routledge.

Buckley, W. and Sandkull, B. (1969) *A Systems Study in Regional Inequality: Norrbotten, a Fourth of Sweden*, Stockholm: SIAR.

Burns, T. and Stalker, G. M. (1961) *The Management of Innovation*, London: Tavistock.

Burrell, G. and Cooper, R. (1988) 'Modernism, Postmodernism and Organizational Analysis: An Introduction', *Organization Studies*, 91–112.

Burrell, G. and Morgan, G. (1979) *Sociological Paradigms in Organisational Analysis*, London: Heinemann Educational.

Calás, M. and Smircich, L. 1991, 'Voicing Seduction to Silence Leadership', *Organization Studies*, 567–601.

Carlson, S. (1991) [1951] 'Executive Behaviour', reprinted with contributions by Henry Mintzberg and Rosemary Stewart, *Acta Universitatis Upsaliensis, Studia Oeconomiae Negotiorum*, 32, Stockholm: Almqvist and Wiksell International.

Carlzon, J. (1985) *Riv Pyramiderna*, Stockholm: Bonniers.

——(1987) *Moments of Truth*, Cambridge MA: Ballinger.

Chanlat, J-F. (1994) 'Francophone Organizational Analysis (1950–90): An Overview', *Organization Studies*, 47–80.

Chen, C. C. and Meindl, J. R. (1991) 'The Construction of Leadership Images in the Popular Press: The Case of Donald Burr and People's Express', *Administrative Science Quarterly*, 36, 521–51.

Clegg, S. (1990) *Modern Organisations: Organisation Studies in the Postmodern World*, London: Sage.

Collins, R. (1979) 'The Politics of Professions', in R. Collins (ed.) *The Credential Society*, New York: Academic Press.

Cooper, R. (1986) 'Organising/Disorganising', *Social Science Information*, 25: 2, 299–335.

——(1988) 'Modernism, Post Modernism and Organizational Analysis 3: The Contribution of Jacques Derrida', *Organization Studies*, 479–502.

Cyert, R. M. and March, J. G. (1963) *A Behavioral Theory of the Firm*, Englewood Cliffs NJ: Prentice-Hall.

Czarniawska-Joerges, B. (1988) *Att Handla med Ord (To Coin a Phrase)* Stockholm: Carlssons.

——(1992a) *Styrningens Paradoxer (Paradoxes of Management)* Stockholm: Norstedts Juridikförlag.

——(1992b) *Exploring Complex Organizations: Toward an Anthropological Perspective*, Newbury Park CA: Sage.

——(1993) *The Three-Dimensional Organization: A Constructionist View*, Lund: Studentlitteratur/Chartwell Bratt.

Czarniawska, B. and Joerges, B. (1996) 'Travels of Ideas', in B. Czarniawska and G. Sevón (eds) *Translating Organizational Change*, Berlin: de Greuter, 13–48.

*Dagens Nyheter*, 6 August 1964.

Danborg, T, Hammar, G. and Lind, J-I. (1975) *Region i Kris: Samhällsorganisatorisk Diagnos av Sydöstra Skånes Växtproblem (Region in Crisis: A Social Organisational Diagnosis of the Growth Problems in South-East Scania)* Lund: Studentlitteratur.

Deal, T. E. and Kennedy, A. A. (1982) *Corporate Culture*, Reading MA: Addison-Wesley.

De Man, H. (1995) 'Universities and Management Education in the Netherlands: The Reception and Transformation of the Idea of the Academic Business School', paper presented at the EMOT workshop 'Production, Diffusion and Consumption of Management Knowledge in Europe', held at IESE, Barcelona, 26–8 January.

DiMaggio, P. and Powell, W. (1983) [1991] 'The Iron Cage Revisited: Institutional Isomorphism and Collective Rationality', in W. Powell and P. DiMaggio (eds) *The New Institutionalism in Organizational Analysis*, Chicago IL: University of Chicago Press, 63–82.

——(eds) (1991a) *The New Institutionalism in Organizational Analysis*, Chicago IL: University of Chicago Press.

——(1991b) 'Introduction', in W. Powell and P. DiMaggio (eds) *The New Institutionalism in Organizational Analysis*, Chicago IL: University of Chicago Press, 1–40.

Edgren, J., Rhenman, E. and Skärvad, P-H. (1983) *Divisionalisering och Därefter: Erfarenheter av Decentralisering i Sju Svenska Företag (Divisionalisation and Afterwards: Experiences of Decentralisation in Seven Swedish Companies)* Stockholm: Management Media.

Engwall, L. (1992) *Mercury Meets Minerva*, Oxford: Pergamon.

——(1998) 'Mercury and Minerva: A Modern Multinational', in J-L. Alvarez (ed.) *The Diffusion and Consumption of Business Knowledge*, London: Macmillan, 81–109.

Engwall, L., Furusten, S. and Wallerstedt, E. (1993) 'Bridge Over Troubled Water', paper presented at the 11th EGOS Colloquium in Paris, 6–8; Working Paper 1993/4, Uppsala University: Department of Business Studies (revised version 1997, mimeo).

Ericsson, C. (1987) *Utan Omsvep: Mitt Berikande Liv med Consafe (Straight Out)* Stockholm: Timbro.

Fayol, H. (1949) [1916] *General and Industrial Management*, London: Pitman.

Fernler, K. (1996) *Mångfald eller Likriktning (Divergence or Convergence)* Stockholm: Nerenius & Santérus Förlag.

Feyerabend, P. K. (1975) *Against Method: Outline of an Anarchistic Theory of Knowledge*, London: NLB.

Forssell, A. (1994) 'Företagisering av Kommuner' ('Company-ization of Municipalities') in B. Jacobsson (ed.) *Organisationssexperiment i Kommuner och Landsting (Public Organization Experiment)* Stockholm: Nerenius & Santérus Förlag, 22–37.

Forssell, A. and Jansson, D. (1999) *En offentlig reformation. Marknadisering och företagiseringi offentlig sektor* (A Public Reformation), Stockholm: SCORE (book manuscript).

Foucault, M. (1993) [1971] *Diskursens Ordning (l'Ordre du Discours {The Order of Things})* Rönneholm: Brutus Östling Bokförlag Symposium.

Furusten, S. (1992) 'Management Books: Guardians of the Myth of Leadership', thesis, Uppsala University: Department of Business Studies.

——(1993a) 'Kunskap eller Ideologi: en Studie av Populär Företagslitteratur' ('Knowledge or Ideology') *Forskning om Utbildning*, February, 3–22.

——(1993b) 'Mercury Mastering Minerva: The Commercialisation of a Research Oriented Consulting Firm', paper presented at the conference on 'Professions and Management', Stirling, 26–8 August.

——(1996) 'Lets Go Beyond the Myths of Management', in T. Elfring, H. Siggard-Jensen and A. Money (eds) *Theory-building in the Business Sciences: Papers from the 2nd EDAMBA Summer School*, Copenhagen: Handelshögskolans Förlag.

——(1998) 'The Creation of Popular Management Texts', in J-L. Alvarez (ed) *The Diffusion and Consumption of Business Knowledge*, London: Macmillan, 141–63.

Furusten, S. and Hallström, T. (1996) 'Standards and Standardization', paper presented at 3rd EURAS Conference, Standards and Society', Stockholm, 5–7 May.

Furusten, S. and Kinch, N. (1992) 'Swedish Managerial Thinking: A Shadow of America', in R. Lundén and E. Åsard, E. (eds) *Networks of Americanization: Aspects of the American Influence in Sweden*, Uppsala, Acta Universitatis Upsaliensis: Almqvist & Wiksell, 55–79.

——(1996) 'Scandinavian Management, Where are You?', in S. Jönsson (ed.) *Perspectives on Scandinavian Management*, Göteborg: GRI.

Geneen, H. (1985) *Managing*, London: Grafton.

Giddens, A. (1988) [1979] *Central Problems in Social Theory*, London: Macmillan Educational.

——(1991) *Modernity and Self-Identity*, Oxford: Polity Press.

Greiner, L. and Metzger, R. (1983) *Consulting to Management*, Englewood Cliffs NJ: Prentice-Hall.

Gulick, L. and Urwick, L. (eds) (1937) *Papers in the Science of Administration*, New York: Institute of Public Administration, Columbia University.

Gummesson, E. (1991) *Qualitative Methods in Management Research*, Newbury Park CA: Sage.

Hammer, M. and Champy, J. (1993) *Reengineering the Corporation: A Manifesto for Business Revolution*, New York: Harper Business.

Hasselbladh, H. (1995) 'Lokala Byråkratiseringsprocesser: Institutioner, Tolkning och Handling' ('Local Bureaucratization: Institutions, Interpretation and Action') dissertation, Uppsala University: Department of Business Studies.

Hofstede, G. (1980) 'Motivation, Leadership and Organization: Do American Theories Apply Abroad?', *Organizational Dynamics*, summer, 42–63.

——(1990) 'The Cultural Relativity of Organizational Practices and Theories', in D. C. Wilson and R. H. Rosenfeld, *Managing Organizations' Text: Readings and Cases*, New York: McGraw Hill.

Huczynski, A. A. (1993) *Management Gurus*, New York: Routledge.

Iacocca, L. (1984) *Iacocca: An Autobiography*, New York: Bantam.

Ingersoll, V. and Adams, G. (1992) 'The Child is "Father" to the Manager: Images of Organizations in US Children's Literature', *Organization Studies*, 497–519.

Jackson, B. (1994) 'Management Gurus as Guarantor: The Implications and Challenges for Management Research', paper presented at the British Academy of Management annual conference, Lancaster University, 13 September.

Jepperson, R. (1991) 'Institutions, Institutional Effects and Institutionalism', in W. Powell and P. DiMaggio (eds) *The New Institutionalism in Organizational Analysis*, Chicago IL: University of Chicago Press, 143–63.

Karlöf, B. (1985) *Strategins Kärnfrågor, (Business Strategy in Practice)* Malmö: Liber.

—— (1987) *Strategins Kärnfrågor*, Malmö: Liber.

—— (1988) *Affärsstrategier*, Stockholm: Affärsvärlden Förlag.

Karlöf, B. and Söderberg, S. (1989) *Ledarutmaningen*, Stockholm: Svenska Dagbladet Förlag.

Kennedy, C. (1991) *Guide to the Management Gurus: Shortcuts to the Ideas of Leading Management Thinkers*, London: Business Books.

Kets de Vries, M. and Miller, D. (1987) 'Interpreting Organizational Texts', *Journal of Management Studies*, 24 (3) May, 233–47.

Kilduff, M. (1993) 'Deconstructing Organizations', *Academy of Management Review*, 18, 1, 13–31.

Kimberly, J. R. (1980) 'Initiation, Innovation and Institutionalization in the Creation Process', in J. R. Kimberly and R. H. Miles (eds) *The Organizational LifeCycle*, San Fransisco CA: Jossey-Bass, 18–43.

Kinch, N. (1993) 'Management – Faith or Science? The Popularization of American Management Thinking', in S-E. Brodd (ed.) *Stewardship, Management Ethics and Ecclesiology*, Uppsala: Church of Sweden Research Department.

Kinch, N., Wedlin, L. and Fili, A. (1998) 'CEOS as Carriers of Managerial Knowledge: How do Swedish Managers Talk in Videos Distributed to Employees?', paper presented at subtheme 7, 'The creation and diffusion of management practices', at the 14th EGOS Colloquium, Maastricht University, The Netherlands, 9–11 July.

Kostera, M. (1995) 'The Modern Crusade: The Missionaries of Management Come to Eastern Europe', *Management Learning*, 26, 3, 331–52.

Kragelund (1992) 'Den Akademiska Världens Litteratur om Företagsledning' ('The Academic Literature on Management') term paper, Department of Business Studies, Uppsala University (mimeo).

Kuhn, T, S. (1970) [1962] *The Structure of Scientific Revolutions*, Chicago IL: University of Chicago Press.

Läckgren, C., Westerling, J. and Öberg, M. (1989) 'Managementkonsultbranschen: en Snårskog av Herrar och Slavar' ('The Management Consultant Industry: A Thicket of Masters and Slaves') term paper, Department of Business Studies, Uppsala University (mimeo).

Larson, M. S. (1977) *The Rise of Professionalism*, Berkeley CA: University of California Press.

Latour, B. (1987) *Science in Action*, Bristol: Open University Press.

Lawrence, P. R. and Lorsch, J. W. (1967) *Organization and Environment*, Cambridge MA: Harvard Graduate School of Business Administration.

Lind, J-I. and Rhenman, E. (1989) 'The SIAR School of Strategic Management', *Scandinavian Journal of Management*, 5, 3, 167–76.

March, J. and Simon, H. (1958) *Organizations*, New York: Wiley.

March, J. G. and Olsen, J. P. (1976) *Ambiguity and Choice in Organizations*, Bergen: Universitetsforlaget.

McCloskey, D. (1986) *The Rhetorics of Economics*, Brighton: Harvester Press.

McCormack, M. H. (1984) *What They Don't Teach You at Harvard Busniess School*, Glasgow: Collins.

McGill, M. E. (1988) *American Business and the Quick Fix*, New York: Henry Holt.

McGregor, D. (1960) *The Human Side of Enterprise*, New York: McGraw-Hill.

Meyer, J. (1994) 'Rationalized Environments', in R. Scott and J. Meyer (eds) *Institutional Environments and Organizations*, London: Sage, 28–54.

——(1996) 'Otherhood, the Promulgation and Transmission of Ideas in the Modern Organizational Environment', in B. Czarniawska and G. Sevón (eds) *Translating Organizational Change*, Berlin: de Greuter, 241–52.

Meyer, J. W. and Rowan, B. (1991) [1977] 'Institutionalized Organizations: Formal Structure as Myth and Ceremony', in W. Powell and P. DiMaggio (eds) *The New Institutionalism in Organizational Analysis*, Chicago IL: University of Chicago Press, 41–62.

Mintzberg, H. (1973) *The Nature of Managerial Work*, New York: Harper and Row.

——(1983) *Structure In Fives: Designing Effective Organizations*, Englewood Cliffs NJ: Prentice Hall.

——(1990) 'Strategy Formation: Schools of Thought', in J. W. Fredrickson (ed.) *Perspectives on Strategic Management*, New York: Harper and Row, 105–235.

## 182  Bibliography

——(1991) 'Managerial Work: Forty Years Later', in S. Carlson, *Executive Behaviour* (reprint of the 1951 edition) *Acta Universitatis Upsaliensis, Sturia Oeconomiae Negotiorum*, no. 32, 97–111.

Morgan, G. (1983) 'Toward a More Reflective Social Science', in G. Morgan (ed.) *Beyond Method*, London: Sage, 368–76.

——(1986) *Images of Organization*, Beverly Hills CA: Sage.

Norberg, L. (1987) *Känn dig som Ledare*, Stockholm: Timbro.

Normann, R. (1969) 'Variation och Omorientering: En Studie av Innovationsförmåga' ('Variation and Reorientation: A Study in Innovative Ability') thesis, Stockholm: SIAR.

——(1970) *A Personal Quest for Methodology*, Stockholm: SIAR-19.

——(1971) 'Organizational Innovativeness: Product Variation and Reorientation', *Administrative Science Quarterly* 16, 2, 203–15.

——(1975) *Skapande Företagsledning (Creative Management)* Lund: Aldus.

——(1976) *Management and Statesmanship*, Stockholm: SIAR.

——(1977) [1975] *Management for Growth*, Chichester: Wiley.

——(1984) *Service Management*, Chichester: Wiley.

——(ed.) (1989) *Invadörernas Dans (Dance of the Invaders)* Malmö: Liber.

——(1991) [1983] *Service Management*, Malmö: Liber.

Normann, R. and Ramirez, R. (1994) *Designing Interactive Strategy: From Value Chain to Value Constellation*, Chichester: Wiley.

Ödman, P-J. (1979) *Tolkning, Förståelse, Vetande (Interpretation, Understanding and Knowing)* Stockholm: AWE/Gebers.

Olofsson, C. (1969) 'Produktutveckling: Miljöförankring' ('Product Development: Environmental Aspects') thesis, Stockholm: SIAR-S22.

Ong, W. J. (1982) *Orality and Literacy: The Technologising of the Word*, London: Routledge.

Perrow, C. (1986) *Complex Organizations: A Critical Essay*, New York: Random House.

Peters, T. (1987) *Thriving on Chaos*, New York: Knopf.

——(1989) *Thriving on Chaos*, London: Macmillan.

Peters, T. and Waterman, R. (1982) *In Search of Excellence*, New York: Harper and Row.

Pettigrew, A. M. (1975) 'Towards a Political Theory of Organizational Intervention', *Human Relations*, 28, 191–208.

Pfeffer, J. (1981) 'Management as Symbolic Action: The Creation and Maintenance of Organizational Paradigms', in B. M. Staw, and L. L. Cummings (eds) *Research in Organizational Behaviour*, vol. 3, Greenwich CT: JAI.

Pfeffer, J. and Salancik, G. R. (1978) *The External Control of Organizations: A Resource Dependence Perspective*, New York: Harper and Row.

Pickens, Boone T. (1987) *Boone: T. Boone Pickens Jr*, Boston MA: Houghton Mifflin.

Pondy, L. (1978) 'Leadership is a Language Game', in J. McCall and M. M. Lambardo (eds) *Leadership: Where Else Can We Go?*, Durham NC: Duke University Press, 87–101.

Porter, M. E. (1985) *Competitive Advantage: Creating and Sustaing Superior Performance*, New York: Free Press.

Rhenman, E. (1968) *Organisationsplanering: En Studie av Organisationskonsulter (Organisational Planning: A Study of Organisation Consultants)* Stockholm: Läromedelsförlagen.

——(1969) *Centrallasarettet (The Central Hospital)* Lund: Studentlitteratur.

——(1973a) *Organisation Theory for Long-Range Planning*, London: Wiley.

——(1973b) *Managing the Community Hospital: A Systems Analysis*, London: Saxon House.

——(1974) [1969] *Företaget och dess Omvärld: Organisationsteori för Långsiktsplanering (The Firm and its Environment: Organization Theory for Long-Range Planning)* Stockholm: Bonniers.

Rhenman, E. and Stymne, B. (1964) *Företagsledning i en Föränderlig Värld (Management in a Changing World)* Stockholm: Aldus.

Risling, A. and Svejby, K-E. (1986) *Kunskapföretaget*, Malmö: Liber.

Robbins, A. (1987) *Unlimited Power*, New York: Fawcett Crest.

Roberts, W. (1989) *Leadership Secrets of Attila the Hun*, New York: Warner Books.

Røvik, K-A. (1996) 'Deinstitutionalization and the Logic of Fashion', in B. Czarniawska and G. Sevón (eds) *Translating Organizational Change*, Berlin: de Greuter, 139–72.

——(1998a) 'The Translation of Popular Management Ideas: Towards a Theory', paper presented at subtheme 7 'The Creation and Diffusion of Management Practices', at the 14th EGOS Colloquium at Maastricht University, The Netherlands, 9–11 July.

——(1998b) *Moderne Organisasjoner (Modern Organisations)* Bergen-Sandviken: Fagbokforlaget.

Sahlin-Andersson, K. (1996) 'Imitation by Editing Success: The Construction of Organizational Fields', in B. Czarniawska and G. Sevón (eds) *Translating Organizational Change*, Berlin: de Greuter, 69–92.

Sandkull, B. (1970) 'Innovative Behavior of Organizations: The Case of New Products', Ph.D. dissertation, Lund: Studentlitteratur.

Schein, E. H. (1985) *Organizational Cultures and Leadership: A Dynamic View*, San Fransisco CA: Jossey-Bass.

——(1988) *Process Consultation, Volume I: Its Role in Organization Development*, Reading MA: Addison-Wesley.

Schön, D. (1983) *The Reflective Practitioner*, New York: Basic Books.

Scott, R. (1991) 'Unpacking Institutional Arguments', in W. Powell and P. DiMaggio (eds) *The New Institutionalism in Organizational Analysis*, Chicago IL: University of Chicago Press, 164–82.

Scott, R. (1995) *Institutions and Organisations*, London: Sage.

Scott, R. and Meyer, J. (1991) [1983] 'The Organization of Societal Sectors: Propositions and Early Evidence', in W. Powell and P. DiMaggio (eds) *The New Institutionalism in Organizational Analysis*, Chicago IL: University of Chicago Press, 108–40.

## 184    Bibliography

———(eds) (1994) *Institutional Environments and Organisations: Structural Complexity and Individualism*, London: Sage.

Sculley, J. (1988) *Odyssey: Från Pepsi till Apple, (Odyssey: From Pepsi to Apple)* Stockholm: SvD.

Selznick, P. (1984) [1957] *Leadership and Administration*, Berkely CA: Harper and Row.

Senge, P. (1990) *The Fifth Discipline: The Art and Practice of the Learning Organization*, New York: Doubleday.

Sharma, D. D. (1987) 'Internationalization and Technology Transfer: Swedish Management Consultants in ASEAN', in J. Selmer and T. Long (eds) *Economic Relations between Scandinavia and ASEAN*, Stockholm: Stockholm University Press, 241–64.

*SIAR Alumni Register*, Stockholm: SIAR.

SIAR (1975) *Management Survey of UNICEF*, Stockholm: SIAR.

Smircich, L. and Morgan, G. (1982) 'Leadership: The Management of Meaning', *Journal of Applied Behavioural Studies*, 18, 257–73.

Söderlund, M. (1989) 'EFI 60 år: Historien om ett Forskningsinstitut' ('60 Years of EFI: The History of a Research Institute') in *EFIs Årsbok 1989 (EFI Yearbook 1989)* 29–84.

Stewart, R. (1988) [1967] *Managers and Their Jobs*, Hong Kong: Macmillan.

Strang, D. and Meyer, J. (1994) 'Institutional Conditions for Diffusion', in R. Scott and J. Meyer (eds) *Institutional Environments and Organizations*, London: Sage, 100–12.

Stymne, B. (1970) 'Values and Processes: A Systems Study of Effectiveness in Three Organizations', dissertation, Lund: Studentlitteratur.

———(1995) in L. Engwall (ed.) *Föregångare inom Företagsekonomin (Predecessors in Business Studies)* Stockholm: SNS, 369–94.

Svejby, K-E. and Risling, A. (1986) *Kunskapsföretaget (The Knowledge-Intensive Firm)* Malmö: Liber.

*Svenska Dagbladet*, 5 August 1964; 6 July 1965.

Taylor, F. (1911) *Principles of Scientific Management*, New York: Harper and Row.

Thomas, A. (1989) 'One-Minute Management Education: A Sign of the Times', *Management Education and Development*, 20, 23–38.

Thompson, J. (1967) *Organizations in Action*, New York: McGraw-Hill.

Toffler, A. (1980) *The Third Wave*, New York: Morrow.

*Vem är Det 1993 (Who's Who in Sweden 1993)* Stockholm: Norstedts.

Wallroth, C. (1968) 'Experiences in Organizational Change: Long-Range Planning in a Government Office', thesis, Stockholm: SIAR-13.

Weick, K. (1979a) *The Social Psychology of Organizing*, New York: Random House.

———(1979b) 'Cognitive Processes in Organizations', in B. M. Staw and L. L. Cummings (eds) *Research in Organizational Behaviour*, vol. 1, 279–308.

Whitley, R. (1984a) *The Intellectual and Social Organisation of the Sciences*, Oxford: Oxford University Press.

——(1984b) 'The Scientific Status of Management Research as a Practically-Oriented Social Science', *Journal of Management Studies*, 21, 4, 369–90.

——(1985) 'Knowledge Producers and Knowledge Acquirers', in T. Shinn and R. Whitley (eds) 'Expository Science: Forms and Functions of Popularisation', *Sociology of the Sciences*, vol. IX, 3–28.

Wickström, S. and Normann, R. (1994) *Knowledge and Value: A New Perspective on Corporate Transformation*, London: Routledge.

Willmott, H. C. (1993) 'Breaking the Paradigm Mentality', *Organization Studies*, 14, 5, 681–719.

Wilson, H. T. (1983) 'Anti-Method as a Counterstructure in Social Research Practice', in G. Morgan (ed.) *Beyond Method: Strategies for Social Research*, New York: Sage, 247–59.

Woodward, J. (1965) *Industrial Organisation: Theory and Practice*, London: Oxford University Press.

## Other sources: interviewees

These are listed alphabetically and *not* according to the numbers (R1, R2, R3, etc.) used to designate respondents in the text. All interviews were conducted between December 1992 and May 1993.

Olof Arwidi
Malcolm Borg
Bengt Brodin
Lars Bruzelius
Rune Castenäs
Jan Edgren
Henrik Fock
Christer Kedström
Curt Kihlstedt
Bertil Näslund
Richard Normann
Christer Olofsson
Eric Rhenman
Per-Hugo Skärvad
Sten Söderman
Bengt Stymne
Christer Wallroth

# Index